AF447747

ENCHANTMENT

Gary J. Buehler

Enchantment

Copyright © 2024

By Gary J. Buehler

Cover & book design by Lucretia Alejandre

Published by
New Education Press
www.NewEducationPress.com

ISBN: 979-8-218-41824-3

Printed in the United States of America

dedicated to
the love of my life

CHARLOTTE

and our children

TONJA, TAMMY, AND TODD

and their children

KYLE, ELIZA, HANNA AND GAVIN

with special thanks to

members of my writing groups

*Paul Arndt, Deborah Arndt, Rae-Ellen Kavey, MD,
Melanie Krebs. Joan Pedzich,
and Wayne VanderByl, JD*

advisors, reviewers, copy editor, and publisher

Copy Editor: *Nancy Titus*
Publisher: *Steven Swerdfeger*
Designer: *Lucretia Alejandre*

TABLE OF CONTENTS

Prologue

This third book in my series continues to address the request of our eldest daughter. Her strong suggestion was to have me put in writing a few of the experiences that ended, the majority of the time, in a smile or an unanswered question. One of the enduring questions for ages has always been: why? For some of the tales you will encounter here, I cannot begin to answer the why all these incidents occurred, but I do know the how, the where, and in most cases, the when they impacted my life. This book may be better understood by reviewing my previous writings for a better understanding and for context. The book titles are: *An American Story* and *I Don't Know If It Happened This Way…*

Each of the following stories assist in helping me realize the richness of my life and the role family, friends, hobbies, and work have aided in my enjoyment. Those moments in these stories where and when things could have taken a turn for the worst, could have gone terribly wrong, or run my train off the tracks, a happy ending was not too far distant. Call it luck or something else. I prefer the basic truth: "treat others as you wish to be treated." I have not always lived by the Golden Rule. Where I failed or deviated from this, I failed miserably, even hurt others. Yet I can say it was a learning experience.

Also included in this collection are photos of some of my sculptures, another hobby dear to me. Two of the stories are about specific works I created, which you can see both on the cover and inside. The others are a sampling of sculptures designed and constructed by me over the past fifty years.

I first began to become aware of art constructed of metal by visiting and viewing art works created by renowned Rochester artists such as Albert Paley and Al Wilson during the early 1970s. Shortly thereafter, I tried testing a market for my creations at the Memorial Art Gallery's "Clothesline Art Show," where I experienced some success and realized folks liked my work and were actually were willing to spend their money to take them home. Nothing encourages one more than a person spending their hard-earned money to buy one of your creations. I do not know if this is true for everyone, but it certainly works for me in this scenario.

I like to work with steel because when it is heated to almost its molten state, it can be manipulated, bent, formed, and fused together fairly easily. Also I am inspired by the ways in which metal can be engineered to bring about a change in color by applying heat, oxidation, and various acids. The resulting colors are so vivid that folks have challenged me, refusing to believe some of the colors I have created are a result of techniques used and not from paint. So the challenges continue and keep me motivated to work and to go on creating.

ENCHANTMENT

As a youngster, I fondly recall lying on my back in the tall grasses of a hayfield with the sun warming my face, chest, and torso, summer breezes blowing my hair wild as I watched the puffy, white, cotton-ball cumulus clouds move across the azure sky. The constantly moving scenes before me of horses, people, rabbits, trains, clowns, and drawings were endless in my imagination. The minutes ticked by unnoticed, carefree, and often turned into hours until either my stomach or my name being called from the farmhouse porch told me it was time to come in for lunch. The circus parade for that day ended to return yet another day. It was a magical place in the summer heat of August.

The loft of the barn, filled with hay, became another delight for me. It was a wonderland to play where I could spend endless hours moving the bales around to create places to hide or build little forts to protect me and my cousins from imaginary Indian attacks. Moving the bales around usually caused the twine holding them together to either fray, break, or otherwise degrade the bales, creating untold frustration for my uncle when summer phased into fall, then winter, and he had to move the hay to feed the animals. Every summer we were told to play outside and not in the barn, but the temptation was always too great for me. Yielding to those urges often resulted in severe scoldings and a promise of the warming of our behinds for disobeying. Life lessons were being taught, without our awareness, for making bad decisions and the resulting consequences.

During the school year when not on the farm, life was focused on school and home. Our house where I grew up was within city limits but located rather far out from the center in an undeveloped area. There were still empty lots, fields, woods, and even a pond to play in with my neighborhood friends. In the springtime, flooding in the woods provided us with waterways to explore. Our imaginary ship to sail the seven seas was an old wooden mixing tub used by one of the masons in the neighborhood. It was heavy, made of thick planks. The accumulation of old plaster and cement from years of use clung to its sides and bottom even after being cleaned each time it was used. But it floated and was water tight and it didn't leak! It was very heavy and had to be hauled from behind the neighbor's garage where it was stored standing upright, all the way to the woods and then returned to that same location at the end of each day. It was our navy's only vessel. We all knew the stories of Mark Twain's, *Tom Sawyer* and *Huckleberry Finn.* If a raft and long poles worked for them, then our cement raft tub and long poles surely would work for us. And they did! We explored all the waterways in the woods where our raft would take us with exception of when it was overloaded with too many friends. Trudging home with wet, soggy, muddy shoes or sneakers and carrying our heavy boat did not lessen the joy of our exotic excursions, but explaining why our "school shoes" were wet did dampen the mood just a bit.

The farm and woods seem to have developed an attraction for me. So much so that early on in our married life, my wife and I purchased ten acres adjacent to the same farm where I spent many summers while growing up. We cleared the newly acquired land and developed it, built a road leading into it, and then built a cabin. The cabin was located just above the sloping hillside edge of the pond on the property. My old familiar jaunt became a new location with new fascinations for our family. Our building project reminds me of the saying, "What goes around comes around." It became a favorite place for all of our family.

Onward to today's most enchanted location — for both of us — home! Charlotte's flower gardens and trees abound and delight us throughout the seasons, enhancing sculptures and buildings. Our refuge is complete with the sounds of the lake and waves gently lapping the shore or crashing on break walls or winter ice jams. It's the sound of the wind and waves that lull us to sleep each evening the year round. It's ours to savor, enjoy, hold close and dear. It is peace for our soul and mind. Quietude, tranquility, heartsease, and repose. Welcome to our sweet home!

I've given much reflective thought to the delightful places I've experienced over the years, places that have provided a state of mental and emotional calmness, happiness, a sense of freedom and serenity.

Places that produce peace, positive thoughts, moods, and feelings. And I am grateful for them all and how they have nourished my soul.

Bare on Bear

Preacher Roe said it best: "Some days you eat the bear; some days the bear eats you." Gather in closer my friends and I'll tell you the tale of how I ate the bear.

It all began when I was born into a family of high adventure sportsmen and women who loved to hunt, fish, push boundaries, test limits, and enjoy the rugged back country and forests. This is evidenced by my mother's gravestone in the cemetery in Pultneyville, New York. The memorial stone has etched on it, both a fishing rod and rifle, attesting to her love of adventure and having been a life-long participant in both of these sports. One of her last adventures, when she was well into her 80s, was a successful deer hunt when she shot a nice buck while hunting alone. But I digress from the Bare on Bear story.

For many years, beginning in the 1950s, members of the Buehler family and close relatives would travel to the wilds of Canada to hunt and fish. The favorite destination was the La Verendrye Wildlife Reserve in the province of Quebec. The reserve consists of more than 12,000 square kilometers and is located about 110 miles north of Ottawa. The reserve contains 4,000 lakes and rivers and two huge reservoirs, one of which is the Cabonga. Within this area can be found two First Nation communities. Route 117 cuts through the reserve from the south to the north.

My uncles, Fritz and Paul, started exploring the wild backwoods country and lakes of the reserve with a guide from one of the First Nation communities. The first adventure began with a fishing trip and the following year, a hunting trip for moose.

In the early 1950s, there was only one paved road in the reserve. That was Route 117. The mode of transportation into the heart of the reserve for the hunt was by rail, boarding a train at Coliva that was hauling materials and supplies for the International Paper Company. With the aid of topographic maps and knowledge gleaned from previous trips made, my uncles soon figured out that interior portions of the park that were excellent fishing and hunting areas could be reached by the unimproved dirt roads used by the Paper Company's trucks and equipment. Permission was secured by them to use the roads, provided they yielded the right-of-way to all trucks, equipment, and staff.

So began the annual Buehler family fishing excursions in the wilds of Canada's backcountry. As a young lad, I was on one of those excursions along with my uncle Fritz, his wife, Emma, and their eight-month-old son, Greg. Also along on that trip were my mother and her elderly parents. We stayed in tents. Our beds were made of pine boughs, on top of which were placed our sleeping bags. All of our supplies — cooking equipment and everything else we needed for two weeks — was back-packed in by foot from the road, a half-mile through the woods to the river and into the site we had located and selected to make camp and call "home."

As I grew older, my wife Charlotte and I met other friends interested in fishing, camping, and adventure. I think the emphasis on adventure was my top priority and challenge. We decided to plan an extended sojourn to La Verendrye to fish with our friends, Toni and Serge. Serge was an avid angler so he was excited and "all in" on this adventure. It took a bit of convincing to have Toni agree that this was a good idea for a "vacation."

We rented an old, well-used, canvas-top foldout camping trailer from E-Z Rentals, and I borrowed my uncle Fritz's aluminum boat and motor. Serge and I studied the topographical maps we had, met and chatted with my uncle Paul who knew the area well, and we mapped out the route we were to take to the interior of the Reserve using the one lane dirt roads. We planned to camp at the dam at the Cabonga Reservoir, where a river from the north fed into it.

Serge loaded the boat on the top of his car with the motor, gas cans, fishing gear, gas stove, coolers and other equipment we were taking in his trunk. I planned to tow the camper with my car. We packed supplies in my car also, including five gallons of "white gas" for the Coleman stove and dry ice for the coolers. Then we headed north from Rochester. We drove all day and after traveling the last 75 miles very slowly on the rough and unkept logging roads, we reached the targeted point we had selected on the topographical map. It was the dam at the end of the Cabonga reservoir. We pulled the camper to the top of the earthen dam and set it up for the evening. It was late in the afternoon and darkness was close at hand even though it was still summer, albeit late in September.

We were all hungry and I was volunteered to get the stove set-up and started while Serge grabbed his fishing pole, slipped on a "red and white" spinner lure, ran down to the river, and threw his line in. He shouted, "I got one! It's a huge pike!" Second cast, another hit, and a large northern pike. He came running back up the hill shouting, "This is an excellent spot. We're staying here for the week! Two fish and we haven't even put the boat in the water!" It was soon dark and the coolness of the night was surrounding us.

Our wives offered to walk down from our camping spot to the river with a pail to get water for us so that we could boil pasta for our first dinner. A few moments later they returned out of breath, with a third of a pail of water. They had spilled most of it and were out of breath as well as being scared out of their wits. We asked them what happened, and they told us they heard a snort behind them on the path, a stomping sound and ran all the way back to us. Serge and I took the flashlight and walked down the path. We saw the spilled water in the dirt and also moose tracks going uphill toward the camper.

We settled in, cooked the pasta, ate dinner, packed everything up as it appeared that a storm was moving in quickly. We placed both of our coolers under the overhang of the camper which just happened to be under our pull-out bed side of the camper. The storm arrived after dinner and it was wild with high winds and a driving rain. The camper was shaking and the four of us woke up around 2 a.m. believing the winds were causing the shaking. We chatted a bit, commenting on the high winds, and how much the camper was shaking and hoping the canvas would hold and not tear off from the wind or leak from the pounding rain. Charlotte and I tried to go back to sleep but the shaking continued and several times our bed seemed to lift up a few inches and then drop back down. We both thought it was due to the wind. Finally the shaking, lifting, and dropping stopped. The wind died down, rain became lighter, and sleep overcame us once again.

Morning light came sooner than I wished. I crawled out of bed, pulled on my clothes, slipped into my shoes, stepped out of the camper through the back door, down the single step, and walked by our side of the camper when I stopped dead in my tracks. There before me were several piles of bear scat and our large cooler chest had been dragged out from under the camper. It's lid was open and all our frozen food stuffs and meat were missing. Those bumps in the night, the shaking and lifting of our bed up and then being dropped down a couple of inches, wasn't the wind. It was the bear getting into the cooler! We ate fish the rest of the week. Thank goodness, the bear didn't find our raw potatoes in the other cooler.

The second day, the four of us fished by boat, trolling, and by early afternoon that day and every subsequent day, we had our limit by noon or before. We knew what we were having for dinner that day and for the duration of our stay. Somewhere around the third day, we decided to skip fishing and try to follow the topographical map and see if we could find our way to Maniwaki. Little did we realize the road on the map ended at the town. There was no road leading out of Maniwaki to the north and we returned back to camp the way we came. We finally understood the meaning of the term, "This is the end of the line," but it seemed more like "the end of the world." Perhaps it wasn't really the end of the world, but I am positive I could see the end of the world from the Main Street of Maniwaki!

We never spotted another vehicle or human being the week we were there until Friday. It truly was wild backcountry. On Friday, we noticed three men setting up a tent across the river from where we were camped. We walked down to the shore of the river and shouting across to each other, we shared greetings and answered their inquiries regarding our success with fishing. Then bid each other adieu. Later that evening after dinner, we had a visitor from the encampment on the other side. He was carrying a rifle which made us a bit nervous as well as curious. As we chatted, we noticed that across the river, the two guys appeared to be frying bacon over a wood fire as we could smell it in the air, and that's when we noticed a black bear emerging from the woods, headed directly toward their tent. We started shouting and waving our arms to get their attention. It worked. They then turned and saw the bear moving toward them. Both of them shouted, waving their arms, with the bear still moving toward the frying bacon. At this juncture, the guys ran away from their camp down toward the river bank.

Their other party member, with us on our side of the river, fired a warning shot from his rifle but the bear kept advancing and was not deterred. Two shots later the bear was dead. The campers hung the bear up in a tree, cleaned it, and went back to preparing their dinner. Later that evening all of us had a chance to gather together. We found out that they were going to stay the following week. We shared with them that we planned to leave and return to home to Rochester early the next day. They didn't want the bear to take home because they were worried that it might spoil and not last the week without cooler daytime temperatures. They asked us if we wanted the bear. Silly us — rather silly me — I said I would take it. Serge was certain we'd be able to get it out of the reserve and across the border without any problems.

The following morning we packed the bear in the back of my trunk, then filled the rest of the trunk with all our fishing gear and assorted items, completely covering the bear. Serge packed the cooler with our fish in it in his trunk along with the rest of our gear. We made our plans. I was to follow him, and when we reached the check point of the reserve, I was to stay in the car and he would get out and talk to the warden/gate keeper. We traveled seventy miles on the dirt roads and stopped at the gate. Serge jumped out of his car and started an excited and animated conversation in French with the warden. He opened his trunk and showed the inspector the fish we caught as he continued to explain how great the fishing had been. In the meantime, a dog that had been lying on the porch of the guard shack was now up, sniffing the air, and walking towards the back of my car. Serge noticed the dog and what was happening and started hollering for him to lie down, as did the inspector. Serge wanted to know where we could buy ice for our fish and that we had to get going right away. It worked, and off we were waved through the check point. There were no dogs at the U.S. border crossing at Ogdensburg, New York, that we had to deal with or worry about, and after answering all the usual questions, we were waved through right behind Serge. He chatted in French with the agent and explained his friends were behind him and that we were traveling together. After many more hours of driving, we were back in Rochester.

Leave it to Serge, he arranged for the next steps. He had a personal friend who was a butcher, and he agreed to make arrangements and split the cost of cutting, wrapping and fast-freezing the meat in exchange for half of it. After Serge's phone call back to me, the bear was dropped off Saturday night at the butcher's shop. I left explicit directions that I wanted to save the bear skin so I could have it made into a rug. I arranged to pick up the wrapped and frozen meat packages and the bear skin on Sunday morning. The plan was coming together. Sunday, I did pick up the meat which was in cardboard boxes, but there was an extra box with a closed lid. The butcher opened it up to show me what was in it. It was the head of the bear! He told me he had no way of getting rid of it as he couldn't put it in his waste containers for pick up as it could create difficult questions and trouble he did not wish to invite. It was left up to me to get rid of it! Curses!

During these years, the City of Rochester had a garbage dumping site off Emerson Street in Rochester. Very late Sunday night, I drove out to the dump site. The gates were locked. I drove along the fence, found a spot to throw the heavy box over the fence and then returned back home. A few days later, there was a small article in the city's newspaper about the mystery of a bear's head being found at the Emerson Street dump facility but no indication of where it came from or how it got there.

A taxidermist did make a rug out of the hide for me. It found it's perfect place (for me) on the floor of our bedroom, on my side of the bed. Every morning the first sensation I felt on my bare feet was the bear rug. After a few years, the rug seemed to vanish, almost into thin air it seems. I wasn't surprised and Charlotte was not disappointed. I think I finally caved in under pressure to get rid of it when she was out of town on a trip. Honestly, I do not remember the details of where, when, or how it happened.

"Some days you eat the bear; some days the bear eats you." Not only did I eat the bear, but for several years, I started my day every morning by sitting up, turning on my side of our bed, and standing my bare feet on the rug to start my day.

Boys Will Be Boys

This little ditty falls into the category of the old saying, "Boys will be boys," or more appropriately categorized as, "They are just jerks, and that is not the way we raised them!"

As a young lad, not even in my teens yet, I went with our family to visit relatives in Pennsylvania for the weekend. This meant that I would have all day Saturday to spend with my country cousin. I thought I was a "big deal," being the "big guy from the big city," and I knew everything about life — or I thought I did.

We arrived late on Friday evening after driving for about four and half hours and were greeted warmly. Fairly early on Saturday morning, I awoke to the wonderful aroma of bacon being cooked in a cast-iron skillet on the old wood stove in the kitchen. The ancient farmhouse had no central heating system or furnace, so the entire second floor of bedrooms along with the "new" bathroom were generally cold. However, each of the upstairs rooms had floor registers that could be opened or closed, thereby allowing the heat from the kitchen to warm them. The floor registers were a great way for the kids to spy on the adults below without their knowledge. By peering into the floor register of the bathroom, which was right above the kitchen stove, I observed pancakes being cooked in the big skillet on the wood stove below in the kitchen. Just like a lightning strike, I quickly brushed my teeth, washed my face, pulled on my dungarees and shirt, and was down the stairs like being shot out of a cannon.

After devouring a huge stack of pancakes with maple syrup, and I am sure, a quarter pound of bacon, my cousin and I were out of the house in the barn yard digging for worms. There was no question about what the day held for us. It was going to be a great fishing adventure! We were going to catch some *brookies* (brook trout) from the small creek that ran through the back portion of the farm. After the grand breakfast, the two of us headed out with our fishing poles, a can of worms, and no thought of lunch or the time of day. Both of us were full of enthusiasm and confidence that we were going to provide everyone back at the farm house with dinner that evening.

I would estimate that it was about 9 o'clock in the morning when we started working our way up the creek. Brook trout are not the easiest fish to catch. You have to be an experienced, skilled, and stealthy fisherman. If your shadow shows on the water, your chances of scaring the fish are excellent. Additionally, you must not splash the water as you walk in it. Otherwise, all you are doing is scaring the fish and causing them to seek shelter and to hide in the deep pools of the stream. We were both trying very hard to catch fish, but apparently, the fish had other plans as we excelled at scaring them away.

As the sun reached its apex in the sky, our tummies began to rumble and call to us, "We need food!" We had been slogging for hours through the creek, covering something like two or three miles with no results in catching and landing a mess of *brookies*. But we knew one thing for sure, we were hungry. In fact, we might say we were starving.

Of course, we had not planned or given a thought to bringing anything to eat or to drink with us. We were perfectly happy to drink out of the pristine, clean, and fast flowing creek, using our hands as a cup to scoop up the water. However, that did not solve the problem that we were hungry, and that it was a long hike back to the house. On top of that, we were embarrassed that we had nothing to show for our efforts in bringing home some dinner.

But our more immediate need was food now. I noticed as we had been walking in the creek that right alongside us was a field of corn. So I suggested that we make for ourselves a lunch of corn. I explained the process: we could get some wood, start a fire, soak the corn in the creek, roast it in the fire, and then we'd have a fine lunch. My cousin said we couldn't eat the corn as it was field corn, but I insisted that if it was fully cooked in the hot coals of the fire, it would be delicious — but it had to be soaked in water first. I asked if he had ever eaten corn after it was roasted in a fire. He told me he had never tried it. So, I guess I showed him how much I knew! Then I realized that we did not have a way to start a fire. My country cousin had some wooden matches in his pocket so that problem was solved.

We climbed under the fence or over it, I can't remember which, into the field and we each picked ourselves three of the largest and finest ears we could find. We built ourselves a fire in a spot we created that was circled by large stones we had gathered. We were successful in building a fire as the corn was soaking in the creek. It wasn't long before we had a large pile of red hot embers, and we placed the corn in them, turning them over and over, with a small stick. After the ears of corn were thoroughly cooked and blackened by the hot embers, we retrieved the ears from the fire, peeled off the husks. We thought we would rough it by going without salt and butter, which we did not have with us anyway!

The corn was very tough and not tasty at all, not one bit!

This is when I learned the difference between sweet corn for eating and field corn for feeding animals. No matter how long you roast it or how well it is prepared, field corn is not tasty, and you cannot eat very much of it even if you wanted to. We ended the day without catching a single fish, and we did it all on empty stomachs.

The spaghetti dinner that evening was delicious and no one was surprised that we did not have any *brookies* to be fried in butter in the iron skillet on the cookstove. The adults didn't seem to be too disappointed, but we sure were! I guess I showed my country cousin what a big deal I was and how much I knew about life, fishing, and preparing corn for lunch.

Searching for Answers

Anything I may think, need, or wish to know about, I simply go to my computer and type it in, such as:

How do I replace the gas valve on a Honeywell VR8200?

What is the best way to marinate red onions?

Show me photos of a 1913 Maxwell.

What brand name and quality fly fishing rod should I buy for under $100?

How do I get rid of a tree stump in my yard?

What is the distance to the North Star?

What is a lightyear?

Instantly I have my answer. But it wasn't always this easy. The term *computer* was not in common use nor was it even invented as a machine during the time when I was in public school and even in graduate school! If I wanted to know about something very specific, I had to find the right person to ask and that person had to be someone who knew just about everything there was to know about the specific topic, issue, or question I had. As I reflect back on being a youngster, I recall some of the folks who I thought were wise or knew everything there was to know about what I was trying to understand.

I fondly remember Reverend Booth. I thought he was the smartest person I knew as he was more knowledgeable about the sacred Word than anyone else, even my grandmother who easily memorized so much of the New Testament. Reverend Booth studied both the Bible and the Torah. He was able to pronounce all those words in the sacred texts that I couldn't. In his sermons, he would read the reference or passage in English, and then he also was able to read it in the original language of Hebrew, Greek, or even Aramaic. He would explain the meaning of the word or term in the context of the culture and the age when it was written. I found this fascinating. He could preach for an hour, hold me spell bound, keep me interested, and usually without any notes or written outline. I thought he was very wise and knew everything there was to know about the religious beliefs our family held.

Then there was my Uncle Fritz. He knew everything about mechanical things as well as all types of cars and trucks. Folks would bring their automobile over to him just so he could listen to the engine. He could diagnose the problem every time. He'd raise the hood, listen, sometimes take a long screwdriver and place one end of it on the engine block with his ear on the handle, using it like a doctor uses a stethoscope, and say something like, "It's a stuck lifter on cylinder five." Or "Wrist pin on number three is hammering, probably need the bearings on the rod and crankshaft replaced." Or, "You need new wires from the distributor to the plugs and a new set of points." He was always right!

In high school, I had Mr. Epping for trigonometry. He scared everyone who ever took his class as he seemed to know so much more than what we read and tried to learn from our textbook. From his mind, without looking at charts or reference tables, he wrote the values on the board for sine, cosine, tangent, cotangent, secant, and cosecant to solve the problem on the pages of our textbooks. He would review our homework without referencing the textbook, seemingly from memory. We were so scared of misbehaving there was never an incident of discipline or chastisement for not having done one's homework assignment, save for one incident. And that one time ended with, "Buehler, I feel sorry for you, so very sorry. Now go out and stand in the hall until class is over."

As college rolled around, I found myself seated in a class at the University of Rochester, entitled Physics and Metaphysics, thinking I'm a science major and I can handle this. Wrong! I quickly had to read the writings of Saint Thomas Aquinas, Confucius, Machiavelli, Socrates, Marx, Plato, Schopenhauer, and dozens of others while the professor spoke of them seemingly as his old friends. I was still trying to define, in my mind, how Aristotle, Newton, Gottfried, Bacon, Einstein, and these other friends of the professor were connected as in Metaphysics is connected to Physics. It was a very thick textbook as I tried to figure out the nature of reality, the immortal soul, and the existence of a supreme being, which for me, was a long way from the physics lab and the experiments I enjoyed performing as well as the lab books I that I was correcting for that professor.

What is the point of all of this? Because of my curiosity and wanting to know, wondering, dreaming, thinking, searching, as a pre-teen, I would spend all day Saturday at the Rundell Library in downtown Rochester after taking the bus to get there. Save for the special librarians who took me under their wing, I could never find the answer I was seeking on my own. It usually started this way.

"Can I help you?"

"Yes. I would like to know what E=mc^2 means?"

"Come with me. This is the card catalog. Here are the 'E's,' here is Einstein. Write these numbers down on the paper. Come with me, I'll show you where to find these books on the shelves."

I would wind up with a great pile of books at a table and spend the rest of that Saturday looking at the pictures, diagrams, and reading. After some time had passed, invariably that same librarian would come over to see how I was doing and ask if I needed any more assistance. She usually had a pamphlet, magazine, or yet another book to offer me and added, "This may help you to find what you are looking for."

What a leap from those special memories and days to today, to my desk, computer, or cell phone. I can only wonder if it had been that easy and quick to find the answers then, how could or would that have affected me in the course of my lifelong learning quest and the need to know?

By the way, I can't find the answer to that question on my computer or cell phone, but excuse me for a minute while I read this text message I just received . . .

We Got it All on Tape

Dean, the fire chief in the small community where I was the superintendent of schools, had set up an appointment through the office secretary to meet with me. Prior to the meeting, I asked the secretary what the issue or topic was as I wanted to be as prepared as possible. She really couldn't help me as she had no info or clue, which was very unusual for her. So I prodded along and forward wondering what I was in for.

The chief introduced himself to me, the new guy in town, and began explaining what a great relationship he had with the school district and the gentleman that proceeded me. His introductory history lesson included: how the high school's band always participated in the annual fireman's parade during the school's summer vacation, the number of the school's staff who were members of the volunteer fire department, how complete his department's fire inspection was of all the district's buildings, bus garage, and the inspection of the fire extinguishers, and even offered me an opportunity to become a member since my family now lived in town. I was kind, patient, and tried to be engaged even though I knew there was something more important on his agenda that he hadn't gotten around to yet. My insight was based on instinct and the experience of being the new guy in town. As the coffee in our cups was disappearing, bingo! Surprise! The chief continued on.

"I have a favor to ask. I know the school has a new Panasonic VHS video camcorder, and it is the only one in town. I also know that it is very expensive and the school has a policy of not loaning any audio-visual equipment out. I was wondering if you would make an exception based on the past great working relationship between the department and the district? You see, our department has been holding weekly bingo games for years in order to raise money for a new pumper fire truck. The truck was ordered months ago, and we have just been notified that it is scheduled to be delivered at the end of next week. The members asked me if we could record the arrival of the new vehicle on Saturday as this is a really big deal for all who have been involved in fund raising for so long. I know the camera is big and heavy, so we could also make good use of the tripod. We will assign one fireman to be responsible for it, to operate and care for it, pick it up, and return it to your office. Oh, one other thing, since this a huge event and celebration, almost everyone in town will come out on Saturday and line Main Street when it arrives. It would be nice if the marching band could lead the truck from the edge of town to the bridge on Main where we'll stop, set up the hoses and draw water from the river, and use the pumper to put on a show demonstrating how far and high we can pump a stream of water."

"That sounds like more than one request, Dean. Tell you what, give me some time to think it over. I will need to check with the band director, whoever is in charge of the AV equipment, check our district's policy book, and have a discussion with the board and a few other folks before I can respond to your request. I trust you understand, being I'm the new guy here."

It was a small and tight community I had moved into and I was about to experience a new "J-shaped" learning curve, the kind where you have to fall at the beginning when you don't know things before you can make steady progress upwards. Dean had already covered all the bases before he asked for the meeting with me. I wasn't totally surprised as this wasn't my first rodeo, as the saying goes. I checked all the boxes, and the request cleared all the potential road blocks.

The fire department's appointed video operator picked up the VHS camcorder on Friday. As requested, the school's band marched on Saturday. The new pumper followed the band and stopped at the bridge as planned. Hoses were set, and water was drawn from the river. The new pumper truck sprayed streams of water high into the air and over the bridge into the gorge. It seemed to me that the entire town turned out for the event. I was even in the crowd of spectators that Saturday.

Suddenly, in the middle of the display of the power and capacity of the new tanker, a few folks in the crowd started pointing. Then a few more joined in, until everyone seemed to be focused on the cloud of smoke rising from one of the hills outside of town. The crew quickly shut the truck down, loaded up the hoses, jumped on, turned on all the lights and sirens, and headed out of town towards the rising column of smoke. Then, from the crowd, comments could be heard such as:

"Looks like a big one!"

"Looks like it's up on White Hill!"

"That's about where Ralph's place is!"

"I wonder what he's burning?

Monday morning, bright and early, Dean was at my office with the camcorder in tow.

"Sorry we didn't get this back to you on Saturday as we were all tied up on a fire call. Special thanks for letting the department use the video recorder. It worked out great."

"You are most welcome. By the way, I was there on Saturday and was wondering what caused all the smoke. I noticed you guys packed up quickly and headed out of town."

"Yeah, good thing someone noticed all the smoke. We headed up to White Hill to Ralph's place and his house was entirely engulfed in flames when we arrived. We set up our hoses and were pumping water from the tanker onto the house and out buildings within two minutes after we arrived. It didn't take long before we drained the unit. The fire had already taken his house down to ground level, but we saved all the out buildings and the basement!

We got it all on tape. Want to see it?"

WILD MONKEYS

One important thing I learned in all my years serving as a school administrator was to never go home and leave a tribe of monkeys running free in my office. One may wonder how in the world do monkeys ever get into the school's office in the first place? Well, you see, it is fairly simple, and a game played on unsuspecting targets every day. The target is simply the "boss" or the next person up the list of authority or command.

Here is how it usually works. Someone has a monkey on their back and desperately wants to get it off his or her back. The easiest way to do this is meet and talk with your supervisor and by doing so, if you are really good at it, you then get to leave the monkey there. The parting words spoken by the supervisor should never be any one of the following:

"I'll look into it for you."

"Thank you for sharing this with me, I'll take care of it."

"I haven't run across this before, but give me a bit of time and I'll figure it out."

"Don't worry about it. I'll follow through."

"There is an easy solution as I see it."

"Let me check this out, and I'll get back to you."

"I don't know. Why don't you sleep on it and we'll meet tomorrow."

This is how the monkey gets to stay in the office, by the administrator taking responsibility for solving the perceived problem. One spring afternoon, after 4 p.m., sitting alone in my office, there was a knock on the door followed by, "Do you have a minute, I need to talk with you."

Building Principal: The custodians are complaining about the cafeteria food, the menu, and what's being served to the students. They can't clean the cafeteria as it takes too much of their time.

Me: Really?

Principal: Helen, the cafeteria manager, insists on serving creamy mashed potatoes and gravy and claims the students love them. She can't change the menu because she needs to serve the potatoes with gravy as a way of using our district's allotment of surplus foods from the U.S. Department of Agriculture and to reduce our district's costs of preparing the lunches. Helen explained to me the process she uses to provide earthy richness and wonderful texture: the kitchen staff boils the potatoes with the skins on and then roasts them in the oven before mashing them. The kitchen lunch ladies save the grease from the ground beef that is used for either the meatloaf or hamburgers to make the gravy and also use the surplus USDA butter in the gravy recipe. I've asked Helen to change the menu and stop serving potatoes and gravy. She refuses do so. I believe we need to take them off the menu. I need your support to back me up and have Helen make this common sense, realistic change in the menu.

Me: Really?

Principal: Yes! Why don't you ride over with me to the school, and I'll show you the reason why we need to get Helen to change her menu.

We arrived at the school after the students had left for the day and the custodians were busily cleaning the hallways and classrooms. The cafeteria was empty and apparently hadn't been cleaned yet for the day, and the custodians were working overtime on weekends to clean once every week! As we opened the doors and walked in, I thought I was walking into Mammoth Cave at the National Park in Kentucky. The entire ceiling, every square yard of it, had at least one stalactite hanging down from it. The students had made a game of taking the wrapper off their straws, twisting the end and dipping it into the thick gravy, putting it back on the straw and blowing it with a big puff of air sending it straight up to the ceiling. All the paper wrapper stalactites appeared to be held in place by a small spot of a brown substance. Ahh, Helen's wonderful brown gravy recipe was the magic that made this all possible!

Principal: See the problem? We need to change the menu, and

               Helen will not listen to reason or to me.

Thinking silently to myself, *I see the monkey here on his back and that monkey can't wait to jump on my back.*

Me: I think, perhaps starting tomorrow, you may wish to

               spend all three student lunch periods here in the

               cafeteria with your cafeteria staff and your students.

My "suggestion" wasn't received well as it was more of a directive that would place responsibility squarely on the shoulders of the principal. It was most evident he wanted to avoid responsibility at all possible costs and take the easy way out by eliminating the gravy factor. The monkey was stuck on the principal's back and wasn't going to let go. I certainly didn't want the monkey riding back in the car with me to my office.

It wasn't long after that fateful visit that I realized those heavenly flavorful mashed potatoes were being served without gravy but instead with a pat or two of butter. Nary a complaint reached my office from either the students, parents, faculty, custodians, or cafeteria staff about the missing gravy. Apparently, the principal worked out an agreement with Helen over the switch made from gravy to butter.

And the monkeys all disappeared like magic.

THE BARK IS WORSE THAN THE BITE

It wasn't my first walk around the block. Actually I had been around this block a total of four times in a twenty-year period. This tale relates to the third superintendency of my career. But new positions should never be considered a walk in the park. In any event, here I was, sitting with Bill, the assistant superintendent of business in the school district, shortly after having been appointed as the school board's new superintendent. The ink was barely dry on my contract. As was my usual practice, I had set up individual meetings with each administrator in the district to introduce myself, get to know each of them a little bit, and try to assess "the lay of the land" so to speak.

I liked Bill right from the start. A no-nonsense, focused, no-BS, just-the-facts kind of numbers guy, student focused, experienced and dedicated. After an hour together, Bill's only concern was, "I hope it is OK with you if I take two days of vacation during November, unannounced, weather dependent?" My response was, "Sure Bill, but tell me a little bit more about 'weather dependent'?" Bill shared with me that his passion was deer hunting and he liked to go out in the woods on cold rainy or snowy days, the worst possible weather the better, and hence he couldn't pick the days ahead of time not knowing what the weather was going to be. Bill said he had this agreement with the previous superintendent, and it was the only time during the school year when he would take these two days of vacation time. All other times he would be at work. Looking back over two decades, I can say without reservation, Bill was the best and most competent business person I had the pleasure of working with. To this day, Bill and I are still good friends.

As for the rest of our hour together, Bill shared experienced insights, history, knowledge, and the workings of the district, not the least of which was regarding the board of education. I inquired about each board member, and Bill thought it was important and relevant to acknowledge that the newest member, Frank, just elected, had been the chair of a community tax group. The group had been operational for a couple of years and was concerned about "run-away, out-of-control" town and school taxes. It was Bill's opinion that Frank was elected in a landslide victory with the tax group's support.

Within two weeks, I was faced with my first school board meeting. It ran smoothly, efficiently, and was very cordial. Obviously I had met with the board before this meeting when I had been interviewed twice, then had a dinner together with my wife and board members and their spouses. But this was my first official meeting after being hired. After we had adjourned the meeting, Frank requested that we all stay around for a couple of extra minutes as he had something to say informally. As I recall Frank's comments, they went something like this, "Welcome to the district. We are glad you are here. We look forward to working with you, but I need to tell you something upfront.

I will never vote in favor of a teacher contract with a salary increase in it, an administrative contract with a salary increase in it, or a salary raise for you. Just so you know where I'm coming from and what I stand for, so we don't have any misunderstandings." I wanted to say, "Thanks for that Frank welcome!" but I bit my tongue, smiled, and let it go.

Time has a way of marching on. That first year with the board, Frank was true to his word, being the watchdog of taxes. Frank voted yes on the school budget with a modest two percent increase, no on the new teacher contract with salary increases, no on the civil servants' contract with salary increases. The second year, the board extended my contract two additional years with a generous salary increase. At the public meeting when it came time for the vote, Frank requested we take two votes and the board agreed. The first vote on extending my contract two more years was approved unanimously. The second vote was for the salary increase, and, no surprise, Frank voted no. Frank stayed after the meeting was adjourned and came up to me, and as I can best remember said, "Dr. B., I like the job you are doing here. I hear good things from the teachers, principals, parents, and students. Nothing personal on your salary increase, as you know I told you when we hired you." This time I did not bite my tongue. As best as I can remember, I replied, "I know Frank, no hard feelings. You are a man true to your word. I respect you for that. I do not agree with you on the point of contract salary increases. Please remember that the staff, teachers, and administrators are also members of our community and pay taxes." We shook hands. It was a very firm handshake.

Later one early — I mean very early — morning, I was in the coffee shop having a cup trying to decide if I should close school for the day. In walks Frank. He made some kind of comment about the boss being up early, and everyone at the counter laughed. I offered him a donut and a cup, and asked him what he thought about the weather. "Good for snowmobiling! Do you snowmobile?" I answered him, "Never have but I need to go." I honestly do not remember if we had a "snow day" that morning or not. But time marches on. Soon after that shared morning coffee day, Frank stopped in my office to say hello. He invited my wife and me to his home on a Saturday for a day of snowmobiling. We enjoyed each other's company. A few more dinners and trail rides followed that winter and spring.

Time marches on. A reorganization plan was developed and presented to the board of education for what I believed would improve educational opportunities and learning for students but would cause some changes for adults. No one likes change, especially when it comes to routines and what you are used to! We discussed this plan for a couple of months and encouraged discussion and information sharing through the local newspaper and radio station. Then it was time to make a decision and vote on the reorganization plan. The meeting room was packed. Speakers came to the front to use the microphone. Everyone was heard in the allotted time set aside for discussion. The board president called for the vote. Frank pulled his microphone up close and as best as I can remember said, "We pay Dr. B a lot of money to give us his best advice and recommendations, I think we should take his advice. I vote yes." And so it went around the table.

For two years Frank had been true to his word and been frugal about spending any of the school district's tax-derived monies on a salary increase for me personally. Now here he was advising his fellow board members to listen to me, take my advice, and vote yes, which meant spending money. Yes, taxpayers' money! And this was coming from the former chair of the taxpayers' committee sworn to reduce spending. What made this happen and why this change of heart in Frank? I would like to think and believe it was my years of building trust with all the board members including Frank, giving sound and consistence advice benefitting all the students, as well as good leadership and service as a committed and dedicated superintendent, residing in the town and district.

It was not the snowmobiling that made this happen, I'm sure.

King of the Hill ... Not!

When I was a kid, we used to play a game called "King of the Hill." The way this game was played was a group of us young kids would run around and find a pile of gravel or dirt, or anything that was piled high, and one of us would run up to the top and shout, "I'm the king of the hill." At this point we all realized that the challenge had been issued, and we would all try to become king of the hill by running up and trying to pull, push, or knock the person off the hill and take his or her place. You can imagine the chaos and the amount of iodine solution — that catch-all disinfectant for cuts and scrapes in those days — which usually followed this craziness.

Allow me to share with you one of the hundreds of times in my career where I've been knocked off my hill and humbled, very humbled.

As I was building my career, I thought that once I achieved the position of school administrator and then superintendent I would be somewhat invincible, complete with all the proper respect that comes with the status of the title. Not true, not to be, and not what I experienced!

One such example came after just one year in a small rural northern New York State district serving as the high school principal. I had been selected from a field of dozens of applicants, which was finally filtered down to a group of five finalists. Then I had been chosen and hired! I thought that I had "finally arrived." I was now the district's educational leader. Wrong, oh so wrong! What I had yet to realize, and was to find out later, was that I had become the personal school bus driver/chauffeur of the board of education.

Here is how it all unfolded and how this lofty position was introduced to me. As I mentioned, I was the new superintendent in the district. Early in the fall of my first year, I received a letter inviting me and all the members of the board to attend a county-wide dinner meeting. It was to be hosted by that area's cooperative educational superintendent and the president of the school boards association for all school districts in the county. It sounded like an important meeting, so naturally I shared the invitation with the board, placing it on the next board meeting's agenda. When we arrived at that item on the agenda, with very little discussion, all the members indicated they wished to attend. The motion passed unanimously.

It was at this point in the meeting when the members turned to me and asked if I would be willing to drive as it was several miles distant to the town where the meeting was to be held. Of course I said I would drive, but I did wonder how we all would fit in my car? When I raised the question, that is when I began to learn a bit of history about this small rural district. In the ensuing discussion I learned:

- Most of the county-wide school board meetings were proceeded by a dinner prepared by the culinary students at the cooperative education school.

- To save the district money, it was deemed more efficient to take only one vehicle. This also eliminated the need for each board member to fill out an expense sheet for mileage. The vehicle to be taken was, naturally, the district's school bus.

- To add to the saving of district funds by not having to pay for a bus driver, the practice for years was that the superintendent drove everyone in the district's small yellow short bus.

And that, my friends, is how I became not just the district's new superintendent but also its new school bus driver. But I wasn't finished tumbling down that hill yet. Friends, this is exactly the juncture where I became even more humbled.

It wasn't long after this revelation of my new status that the attorney for the district informed me that continuing this long-standing practice would require me to become a certified school bus driver, or else we would not be covered by the district's insurance. This was several decades ago and at that time in order to be certified as an occasional driver, one of the requirements was I had to have a physical by the school's appointed physician. And so it came to pass, that I signed up on the list of all the district drivers who were required to have their annual physicals. The doctor was scheduled to arrive, and all drivers, including me, were to be examined. The place for the exam would be the high school nurse's office. There was a bit of snickering, many surprised looks, and many questions asked when I entered the office. The exams began and the doctor allowed me to be last.

This part I remember well. Folks that know me well realize I'm a bit of a jokester and like to have a good time and play around a bit when things are not too serious. The office had a waiting area and an inner room where the exams were held. Finally my turn had arrived. The elder German woman doctor invited me in to the room when all the other physicals had been completed. Upon entering, I was greeted and instructed thus: "Remove your shoes, trousers, and shirt, and I will return in a few minutes for your examination."

I did exactly as she instructed. I thought I would make her laugh out loud or, at the very least, smile when she returned. So I took off my shoes, removed my pants, took off my shirt, and immediately put my tie back on and tied a fine knot. Well, don't you know, there was a knock on the door followed by, "Are you ready?" "Yes," was my reply.

The door opened. She looked at me. Not any indication of a smile and perhaps a look of disgust was all I could perceive. The only response I received was, "I need to check your heart rate, so run in place and I will be right back as I have to get my ledger." After several minutes, she returned just as I was almost out of breath and gasping for air. This time I think I detected a slight smile, or perhaps it was a smirk? The doctor's assessment was, "Your resting heart rate is fine, and your higher heart rate is barely acceptable."

So much for trying to be funny. This incident of my own making was another big nudge toward my humility. I also realized who most decidedly was *not* the king of the hill!

Grandpa Days

Gavin, my little guy, was just a bit over three years old and having dressed himself on this particular morning, was asked by his mom, "Why do you have an index card and a pen in your shirt pocket?" His response, "Because I want to be just like Grandpa."

I was semi-retired; my wife, Charlotte, was still working as was our daughter who lived across the street. The three of us hatched a plan together. Each week, Gavin would come over to Grandma and Grandpa's house on Thursday evening to have dinner and spend the night. In the morning, Gavin would have breakfast with both grandparents, then Grandma would leave for work, and Grandpa would have the entire day to spend with Gavin until late Friday afternoon when his mom arrived back home after a day of teaching. Soon the little guy was referring to this day of the week as "Grandpa Day" although in reality, the time was both Grandpa and Grandma Days as we had dinner and breakfast together and in the evenings it was play and reading time with Grandma. It was an opportunity for all three of us to be together with no distractions. I am sure Gavin's mother also enjoyed an evening to herself to relax and catch up with the demands of a busy working woman's life and household responsibilities.

My delightful task was planning what Gavin and I would do for the entire day. Usually we had a destination somewhere in the greater Rochester area picked out to visit in the morning, then we would have lunch at a restaurant, and then drive to a second activity in the afternoon. This allowed an opportunity for Gavin to have a short nap in his car seat while driving to our planned afternoon activity. Some of the fun places we visited included: restaurants, the zoo, shopping malls, toy stores, museums, art galleries, book and art stores, the planetarium, miniature golf, movie theaters, nature walks, playing hide and seek at home, and a zillion other adventures. No stone was left unturned in a 70-mile radius.

While driving in the car with Gavin in the back seat, there was plenty of conversation between us. I called him my backseat philosopher. He seemed to do his best thinking in his child's safety seat. In order to try and not miss anything and remember it all, I always carried a pack of 3x5 cards and a pen in my shirt pocket, so I could record his words of wisdom or observed actions and behavior. Hence his comment to his mom that he wanted to be "just like Grandpa."

We had these days together every week during the school year until he started kindergarten when he was four. I recently revisited the stack of index cards I had accumulated over more than eighty days and went through them to relive the sweet memories and rewarding times of twenty years ago. Wonderful memories of just the two of us. Here are just a very few of them, in Gavin's own words:

I totally love Grandpa Day!

Hey, my sucker is shrinking.

Grandpa, is that a Tyrannosaurs Rex? (It was!)

Grandpa, there are no unicorns in our world, just pumpkins and kittens.

Grandpa, I need to be cleaned up because I have a purple mustache from the grape juice.

Come on, follow me. I'm going to explore.

I forgot something for my mom last night, a big huggy hug.

What did Santa's mother call him?

Grandpa, stop asking me all these questions. They make me frustrated.

Grandpa, if I had a pet frog, I'd name him Leap.

Grandpa, if you hide anywhere where I can't find you, there will be consequences.

Why do they put mummies in coffins in museums?

Have you noticed milk can get sour?

Grandpa, you know what I'm making? A mess.

Grandpa, if you are going to play with me, you are going to have to get up and move around!

Hey, can we go for Chinese for lunch because right next door is a movie theater?

Grandpa, I'm awake, do you hear that chirp, chirp, chirp, and tweet, tweet, tweet?

I called my mom on the phone today but the phone said, "Tammy Buehler is not available."

Grandpa, you are like my mother, but you don't have a girl's voice.

I have to get the sleep out. You know what that means? It means that I have to lay here to get the sleep out of my body before I get up.

Do you know what an egg maker is?

(My reply was yes, a frying pan.)

No, you don't, it's a chicken.

I asked him if he knew what polyester is?

Yes, it's what Shawn is allergic to!

Grandpa, are you happy?

Yes, I replied.

Well, Grandpa, I have fortune cookies at my house and I have one that says if you are happy, you will live longer. So Grandpa, if you are happy, you will live a long, long time!

Will you die when I'm 16?

Hey, it's raining out! Why is it raining out? I know, it's because I said the other day, "Rain, rain, go away, come again another day." Today, it's another day!

Grandpa: he's the coolest guy in the universe!

Every Friday of each week, for two years, was Grandpa Day and on a fateful day, June 22nd to be exact, it concluded. His mother was a teacher and she would be home with the little guy all that summer and The End had arrived. On this day we both realized what this meant for us. We went through our usual planning process for the last day to decide where we would go, what we would do, and where we would have lunch. He didn't wake up at his usual time at 5:45 a.m. but slept until 7:50 a.m. At breakfast, he decided he didn't want to go any place on this morning or even go out for lunch. We stayed home, and after I made his favorite peanut butter and strawberry jelly on toast, he told me he was tired. He lay down on the sofa next to me and drifted off to sleep. It was a quiet ending to a series of exhilarating, adventure-packed days.

The next year he began his public school education in kindergarten, and Grandma and Grandpa began volunteering every Friday at the elementary school he attended. This arrangement continued until he graduated and moved on to the middle school. As his grandparents, we were assigned to assist the teacher and all the children in the same classroom that Gavin attended.

Some two decades earlier, in my wildest dreams and imagination, I could never have guessed that we would have a grandson attending school in the district where I was, at that time, the superintendent. And here we were twenty years later waiting for a different superintendent and the board of education to approve our applications to become volunteers in his classroom.

Strange is it not, the twists and turns that life takes?

CHRISTMAS MEMORIES

Christmas was coming, and I needed money. I had my "working permit" which would allow me to work up to four hours on a school day. I walked into Neisner's on West Ridge Road at the corner of Dewey Avenue on my way home from John Marshall High School. I stopped in to see if they needed any help for the Christmas season. Neisner's, a "5-cents to one-dollar" variety department store, was one of the mainstays of the general merchandise stores in the city at that time, somewhat similar to today's big box stores.

I had an interesting interview with the store manager. First, he asked me if I had my "working permit" and asked to see it. He then asked me if I had any problems lifting boxes weighting up to seventy-five pounds. Next, he wanted to know if I knew how to use hand tools, and if I had a bicycle and knew how to work on it and take it apart and put it back together. I explained to him that I didn't need a bike for work as I attended school nearby, and Neisner's was on the route I took home every day. He took me to the back entrance of the store at the parking lot and then down the stairs to the basement. He showed me the racks filled with boxes of all sizes and told me this would be where I would be working. My job was to pull boxes off the racks and take them upstairs so the sales staff could then stock the shelves. My other job was to carry the items customers purchased out to their cars parked in the lot. "Did I want the job?" "Yes!" I agreed that I would start on Monday afternoon after I got out of school.

I arrived twenty minutes early to meet with the manager and had to wait for him until almost four o'clock. He said, "Hello and welcome" and walked with me down to the basement, showed me the time clock and how to punch in, handed me a small box of tools and pointed out a specific rack of cardboard boxes and told me I could start taking them down, opening them up, and putting them together. When completed, I was instructed to bring each one upstairs, to the store. Before I started, all I noticed were the narrow ends of the boxes on the rack. I pulled the first one down and it was heavy. It was then that I noticed, "Girls, 26-inch, Red." That first afternoon, a total of two bikes appeared on the floor upstairs with another one almost completed, still down in the basement. It was eight o'clock, time to punch out, and I was very hungry as I had had nothing to eat since lunch time at school. I promised myself I would have two lunch bags for tomorrow, one for school and one for Neisner's.

By Wednesday, I was really becoming proficient at the assembly of both the boy's and girl's bikes! The boss came down and asked me to pull another narrow, large box off a different rack. Upon retrieving it, I read the print on the box. It was a baby crib with several pages of instructions packed inside the box. Finally completed, the manager helped me carry it up to the main floor. Then he sent me back to the basement and the bikes once again. The following Monday things changed a bit. Specific requests were coming down from the main floor: a girl's 24-inch red, a boy's 26-inch blue, and so it continued. It started snowing heavily, and the requests to carry bikes and other large purchases out to cars and station wagons increased exponentially. Each trip out to the parking lot and back to the warm basement left me with soaking shoes and cold feet. Arriving home, a bit before nine in the evening, sleep came easily after eating a rather large serving of leftovers garnered from the fridge.

At the end of the first week I was asked to stop by the office after punching out. The manager handed me a small brown envelope, with a flap string wound around a button on it, securing the contents. I unwound the string, pulled out the little piece of paper along with two five dollar bills, a one dollar bill, and shook out the change which amounted to two quarters and two dimes. I looked at the little piece of paper which read: Twenty hours at seventy-five cents an hour minus three dollars and thirty cents for taxes. Total: eleven dollars and seventy cents.

This was my first life lesson regarding taxes.

My grand total for the two full weeks I worked at Neisner's before that Christmas season was twenty-three dollars and forty cents. I was able to repay Grandma the twenty dollars I borrowed from her as an advance for Christmas shopping. I don't remember any of the gifts I bought that year, but I do remember how carefully I shopped, studying catalogs, newspaper ads, and flyers.

The manager told me he didn't need me to work anymore after the holidays but would consider me for next year and thanked me for helping out for this season. In January, I visited Star Markets near my home to see if they were hiring. The manager wanted to know if I had worked at any place else and seemed pleased that I had just finished my job at Neisner's. He hired me for a dollar and twenty-five cents an hour. I was rich! One of my tasks, in addition to stocking the shelves, was to carry out customers' groceries to their cars or station wagons in the parking lot. My wet shoes and cold feet lasted through spring of 1956.

Levi Smoking Jacket

The setting for this tale goes back to the time period of the very beginning of the 1970s. For a few, this "activity" was based on the cultural practices and expectations of the time. It occurred when a few folks were bent on hedonistic "freedom" with little or no perceived restrictions, shame, or consequences. Although marijuana had been around for a long time in our society, it was now viewed by many as a new-found freedom that was being exercised. Although smoked illegally by several folks, including adults and teenagers, it was still not main streamed. For that group, it appeared to be an accepted way to get high, avoid an alcohol-induced hang-over, and participate in a mini-celebration of the Hippie movement.

During this time, I was working in a very progressive school in the city of Rochester. Coincidently, two years earlier, in a different school setting where I was employed, one of the faculty members was caught with marijuana. He was subsequently arrested, suspended from his teaching job and ordered to appear in court. This was all as a consequence of the stringent laws against the use of marijuana. It also should be noted that in the same time frame, many young people, particularly of high school age, smoked marijuana themselves.

Now I thought, wrongly of course, that I was a part of the Hippie movement as my hair was long and my choice of wardrobe was a solid dedication and allegiance to the Levi Strauss Company. That is to say, I wore dungaree pants and jackets most of the time, even in school as did many others.

At that time, my nephews were living with my wife's parents and pretty much being raised by them. One evening, Charlotte and I along with our own children decided to visit Grandma and Grandpa. On this particular visit, I was wearing my favorite outfit. After our visit had concluded, I grabbed my Levi jacket off the coat rack and headed home, never giving it a second thought. I wore that same Levi jacket all week to school each and every day.

On Friday evening, I took off my Levi jacket and hung it in the closet. It was then that I noticed a slight bulge in the front pocket. Upon examination I noticed there was a small plastic bag filled with marijuana, stuffed in that pocket. I was very concerned and showed it to my wife, and mentioned that I had worn it to school all week. I went in the bathroom and flushed the contents of that baggy down the toilet. I was somewhat relieved as I realized what a close call I had survived unscathed. Lucky me!

Later that same evening my nephew called me at home.

Nephew: Hi, Uncle Gary. I think last weekend you took my jacket by mistake, and I took yours. I think we got them mixed them up.

Me: I am pretty sure you are right!

Nephew: Did you find anything in the front pocket?

Me: As a matter of fact I did — after wearing it all week to school every day!

Nephew: What did you do with what was in the pocket, Uncle Gary?

Me: I flushed it down the toilet!

Nephew: Oh no you didn't! Do you know much that cost me?

Me: I don't care what it cost you! Do you know what it means if *you* get caught with that in school? Lucky for *you* that I did not know it was your jacket and what *you* had in the pocket of *your* jacket! *You* are a very lucky man. I'm going to kill you or Grandpa will.

Nephew: Please, please don't tell him or Grandma.

Thereby this true tale ended. To this day, one of my nephews remembers the week without his Levi smoking jacket. And I'm pleased to share, for him it was just a passing fad. I also remember his lament, "Uncle Gary, all the kids smoke!" And my response, "Not *you*! Not anymore!"

HOUSE SITTING IN ALASKA

The landmark 1991 film, *Thelma and Louise,* celebrates two carefree souls piling into a 1956 T-Bird and driving out of town to have sone fun. Then we realize the havoc that is created and subsequence disasters that result.

In the following amazing real-life tale, the protagonists just happen to be my mom Emma, and my aunt Thelma, Mom's first cousin. To round out the other personages, we have George and Susan. George is Thelma's son and Susan is his spouse, and their home is in Fairbanks, Alaska. After college, George, with an earned degree in geology, moved north to work on the Alaskan pipeline, fell in love with the area, stayed, married, and raised a family while finishing his career path at the University of Alaska. Susan worked as a guidance counselor in the Fairbanks public school system.

Thelma often visited her son and his family. Since she was widowed, she desired to have a traveling companion so as not to travel alone. My mom loved to travel and had a special place in her heart for Alaska. So was born the perfect partnership. After several years of Thelma and Emma visiting for a week or two during the summer months, there came a point in time when George and Susan were "empty nesters" and desired to spend their limited vacation time together, not necessarily entertaining Thelma and Emma. They wanted to enjoy the Southern California climate, sun, and surf. It occurred to George and Susan that perhaps the ladies would enjoy house sitting by themselves for a few weeks while they were on vacation. And so the plan was hatched, and Thelma and Emma were now the two carefree souls ready to have some fun out of town. No one could have foreseen how this could possibly unravel, causing havoc and subsequence disasters.

Happily, Thelma and Emma secured their round-trip tickets to Fairbanks and began planning for the three weeks they were going to spend in the log cabin home in Alaska. George and Susan left their Volkswagen Beatle for the ladies to use to explore the Fairbanks area while staying there. Part of house sitting also included caring for their large dog as well as managing the property and home. These expectations were of no concern for the gals as they began making their plans for the many road trips they wished to take while using the cabin as their home base. The planned trips included visits and picnics to state parks and featured a visit to Denali National Park, which is 120 miles north of the cabin.

Thelma and Emma packed the VW for the day and headed out to Denali on typical Alaskan roads. Most folks do not realize how warm Alaska can be on a few rare summer days, and this, I am sure, certainly did not enter into the gals' plans. After many miles and a climb in altitude, challenging the little VW engine, it began to overheat. The driver and passenger were totally unaware of what was happening behind them and the back seat, the location of the little "can do" engine. But as it turned out, it was "no can do" and the smell of hot oil and smoke entered the passenger compartment. As the car pulled over to the side of the road, it was only then that they realized the VW Bug was on fire. The ladies jumped out of the car, grabbing their purses, and stood by helplessly as the flames began to consume the car. The column of smoke and the flames did attract a lot of attention on the sparsely traveled highway, but it was too far from any town or rural fire department's assistance to arrive in time to stop the inferno. The VW literally burnt to the ground before a State Trooper arrived. Thelma and Emma determined to have the car towed back to Fairbanks and put in the driveway at the cabin to await George's return so he could follow through with his insurance company. The gals didn't wish to bother George and Susan while they were on vacation and cause them to worry, so they did not contact them to share the bad news of their tale of woe.

George and Susan returned from their vacation at the scheduled time, called from the airport to be picked up but were told the car wasn't running so they needed to take a taxi home. The gals had the opportunity to share their disaster over the phone but thought it better to do so in person.

Picture the scene. Returning home from a three-week vacation, in a taxi from the airport, and pulling into your driveway to see the burnt-out rusted shell of your VW Bug sitting at the end of the driveway in front of the garage. That was George and Susan's reality! Next, try to visualize walking into your kitchen, facing your mother and your aunt, and asking, "What happened to the car?" After the long story and follow-up questions, the next obvious question was, "What did you do with the dog? Where is he?"

As unbelievable as it is, they had another woeful answer. The fuel oil truck making the summer delivery to fill up the tank for the winter was backing into the driveway when the dog got loose, ran out the kitchen door, barking at the truck, and was accidentally run over. The answer to George's last question was, "She's buried out behind the garage by the garden."

That was the one and only time Thelma and Emma were asked to housesit in Alaska. After that, they continued to be house guests, that's all!

Rear-View Mirror

I'm focused on the passage of time more than I used to be. Perhaps it's due to the celebrations of birthdays for my wife and me as well as our anniversaries. Birthdays come in rapid succession of one another during the dog days of summer, just like clockwork! Our anniversary has passed the double-nickel speed limit by enough years to easily earn both of us a speeding ticket or two. This is what time feels like to me at the moment: I'm in a speeding vehicle and keeping a sharp eye on the rear-view mirror. What have I passed?

The image I see in the mirror appears just after my 16th birthday and comes with the blessing of being able to meet the minimum age requirement for applying for both a work and driver's permit. Next, my 18th birthday and legal freedom from parent's approvals and the opportunity to apply for a loan on my own to buy anything I want, assuming I can afford it, and have the bank's blessing and approval to do so.

Other birthday images flash by in quick succession. What birthday celebration was it when I started college, graduated, got married, started a new career, rented an apartment, had children, had our first new car, bought our first home, was granted graduate degrees, dropped off our children for their first days in kindergarten, in middle school, in high school, met their girlfriends, boyfriends, celebrated their graduations, engagements, marriages, and then, grandchildren, great-grandchildren? All the while, I'm noticing I'm traveling just a bit over the posted speed limit? I haven't seen any flashing red and blue lights in the rear view mirror. I must be okay at this speed! Will I arrive at my destination on time if I keep up this steady pace?

I wonder who'll be there to greet me when I arrive? Will they see me coming up the road, through the trees, and then turning into the driveway? Will they be pleased and happy to see me? Will I have a pleasant meal or maybe just a snack and then dinner out for the evening? Will my room be inviting, comfy, and warm? What are my plans for tomorrow when day breaks?

Did I remember to lock the door of my home and the car out in the driveway as well? We live in a good neighborhood, and this seems like a wonderful one as well, so what is all the worrying about? Let me find restful sleep. It's been an exhausting day and a very long trip. Should I set the alarm for the morning? For what time? Good night . . . sweet dreams my friends. See you in the morning.

Time passes way too quickly when looking in the "rear-view mirror."

L̲OUIS

Sometimes the message catches you off guard and hits you hard, bringing back memories that are delightful, emotional, some too vivid, too recent, and a few you would just as soon remain faded back in the misty haze of memory. What is clear in my mind's eye is the little guy as a toddler, with his baby- blue eyes, sun-kissed feathery blond and silky, wild head of hair. He was the youngest of three, with his sister and older brother rounding out the trio of the young family living across the street from us. That family was now occupying the magnificent twentieth-century brick home that had been in their family for generations. Our daughter was also an adjacent neighbor, in the home next door on the same side of the street, and she often was called upon to baby-sit the little munchkin at various times, thereby creating a tight bond between the two of them and their entire family.

The young man, as he grew, lived his entire life in that beautiful home with his family, through the years of elementary school, high school, college, dating, and marriage. It may sound as if it was an idyllic situation, but sadly, it wasn't. He did graduate *Summa Cum Laude* honors in history with a minor in computer science, was a Winthrop Scholar, a member of national honor societies, Phi Beta Kappa and Phi Alpha Theta. But you see, for three long years, until his struggle ended at age 24, he lived with rhabdomyosarcoma, that's a hideous word. I had to look it up.

Soon after his celebration of life was held, his mom and dad asked me to make a sculpture for them, which I did with honor. That was almost six years ago. Mom and dad moved to the city. Life moves on, as they say, but not easily. We managed to stay in touch.

Then, with no fan-fare an email appeared in my inbox which read:

I have a favor to ask. I know it's been a long time since you created Louis's amazing urn sculpture, but we wonder if you would write a brief story about its creation . . . the meaning behind the various shapes and structure, and also — if I recall correctly how you described it to me — the inspiration for it that seemed to come to you like a shot in the night.

We love having it here with us in our living space, every day and night. And we remain forever grateful to you.

The sculpture did appear in my mind overnight and upon awaking it was "there." I had had the request on my mind for several days and then, "it all came together." This is not unusual as this is the way plans for pieces usually form in my mind before I walk out to the workshop to begin heating, cutting, forming, bending, hammering, and welding pieces of steel together.

My description, starting at the top of the sculpture, with the blue sphere: This was easy for me as it was the color of Louie's eyes. Blue radiates calm, trust, intelligence. It is a serene and calming color, cool, relaxing. Light baby blue is peaceful. Blue stimulates depth, feelings of loyalty, sincerity, wisdom and confidence. It shows stability and faith all wrapped up with wit. The roundness symbolically represents a sense of oneness, wholeness, completion, karma, and energy flow.

Under the blue sphere, are the shiny disks that are akin to the flat figure of a celestial or solar body. As humans, we are attracted to shiny things that serve a purpose for fulfilling our innate needs and fascinated with celestial bodies in our galaxy and the universe.

Next, we have the large steel sphere, shaped just like the earth, holding treasure inside but with no way of reaching it. The geosphere, hydrosphere, atmosphere and biosphere, all parts of the earth, are represented here for family, extended family, and friends.

The treasure of the "earth" is held aloft on the tips of five tall triangles. These trinities can represent: mind, body, and spirt; mother, father, and child; past, present and future; thought, feeling and emotion; creation, preservation and destruction; and if one wishes, the Trinity.

At the base and bottom of the triangles, a light, shining upwards, illuminates the sphere and the treasure it holds. The light is the spiritual symbol of hope and faith, the symbol of a perfect being and immortality. Light eliminates darkness and conveys goodness.

Louis' lighted spirit and goodness lives on in my mind, heart, and soul.

Memory Urn for ashes. Lit in the evening hours.
Welded steel, powder-coated finish.

THE ROAD TO RECOVERY

It was to be an unencumbered and free-spirited road trip, but somehow this plan ran afoul, encountered a road block, and was forced to take a significant detour. So much for the planning which seemed simple enough at first. All too soon, it became complicated when I found myself in a hospital bed, too weak to even turn over on my side, needing help and assistance to accomplish this simple task. I was in a serious state after being unable to move on my own but fortunate to be breathing.

Before the unfortunate incident, our plan was to drive at a fairly leisurely pace, about 400 miles a day, stopping and enjoying the sites along the way, and having a nice meal each evening before retiring to our favorite national chain hotel. The destination we chose was to the city of Tucson, Arizona. We had been to Arizona several times before and always enjoyed Tucson. We had made reservations at a bed and breakfast for our three-week stay. Our main purpose going to Arizona and spending an extended period of time there was to observe and enjoy the desert in bloom. We had always missed this phenomenon on all our previous trips. We also planned to ride some short distances on the fantastic miles of paved biking trails in and around the city, hence the reason for packing our road bikes for this trip. In addition, we planned to walk and hike in the desert and in the multitude of parks and cultivated garden areas. Having enjoyed the Southwest, and Arizona in particular, in past years, we were excited to embrace the spring flowering this year! We were blessed and treated to a rainbow of colors in the desert and mountains as the timing for our visit was indeed perfect!

At the conclusion of our three-week desert stay, we planned to travel to the scenic ruggedness and beauty offered at Big Bend National Park. Since this park is in an area of Texas that is sparsely populated and is a section of our country not often visited by tourists, we had made reservations to stay in an off-the-grid rustic cabin in the park, one of the very few places where overnight accommodations were available. These cabins are so remote that cell service would be spotty or unavailable in this wild area. In hindsight, we were fortunate we were not at this location when tragedy struck as there would have been no way to call for help.

It was a long way to Big Bend from Tucson, so we planned a full day for the drive. However we "played" on the way, stopping in the afternoon when we arrived at the small town of Alpine, Texas. We enjoyed walking around the hamlet, visiting the train station, the city park, and a few of the stores. While on main street after chatting with some folks at the train station, we discovered that one of the trains that was pulling into the station at that very moment was stopping to pick up travelers going to the park. We discovered an old, quaint hotel in town. As we walked around and talked a bit, we decided that we would have dinner in their dining room, as it looked interesting and inviting. The menu was also intriguing. We decided to find out if we could reserve a room, and if we could, we would stay for the evening and leave fairly early (for us) in the morning to drive the rest of the way to Big Bend.

I shall never forget Alpine, Texas! This is where our best-laid travel plans were interrupted and put on hold. My life changed, and so did my wife Charlotte's. It was early in the morning on April 9th, at about 4 o-clock, when the incident occurred. I had what the doctors later determined to be a bilateral stroke. Charlotte called 911, overriding my wishes not to do so. Very shortly thereafter, a team of emergency medical technicians arrived, and the decision was made to take me by ambulance to the only available medical center in the area. I don't remember very much of the panic both Charlotte and I endured, but since then I have been told of the events that took place that morning. Much later that day, a decision was made by the medical staff and Charlotte that I needed treatment that could not be provided at their location. I was in need of much more comprehensive medical services and was airlifted to the University Medical Center in Lubbock, Texas. After being flown 300 miles by helicopter, I was admitted to this hospital. The final medical conclusion indicated that I had suffered a stroke. Several tests were conducted to determine the cause of the stroke with leading indicators being either a heart condition, known as A-fibrillation, or bacteria in my blood stream, which had probably settled on one of my heart valves, causing it to be distributed to the brain with every heartbeat.

Several more tests were conducted, and treatment for sepsis began, a process which was to take six weeks. After a few days in bed, weak and not myself nor feeling well, I was up and shuffling through the halls with a walker. I describe it as walking like a drunken sailor as I was far from being stable on my weak and uncooperative legs and feet. After ten days of observation and a battery of tests, the medical teams decided that I could be released to travel back home to New York State for physical therapy, which should start immediately. Another option was presented at that time, which was the possibility of moving to UMC's partner hospital that focused on stroke victims and their rehabilitation. Charlotte and I opted to go to the South Plains Rehabilitation Hospital also located in Lubbock, pending my insurance company's approval.

At this point in time, I was still dependent on the walker to get around; however, a wheelchair was provided and mandated as I was going to be transported in a medical van. After another ten days in the South Plains Rehabilitation Hospital, participating in physical therapy for three hours each day, it was determined by the medical team that I could be released. I had progressed from wheelchair to walker to a cane to being able to walk a short distance on my own. Although I was approved for release, I still had to be treated for sepsis for four more weeks. This was done by infusion with the drug cefazolin every eight hours around the clock including the many days it would take to get back home. So after 20 days in two hospitals, I was finally going home.

To get home to New York, however, would require another road trip as flying did not appear a viable option. We had our automobile with us, packed for the extended trip, with both our bicycles on the back, but we were still 2,000 miles from our home in Pultneyville, New York. It was a very interesting trip back across the country, and nurse Charlotte was amazing!! Not only did she do all the driving, but she also provided the infusions into my PICC line, a long thin tube inserted through a vein in my arm that ran up to my chest area, near my heart.

Charlotte had an amazing attitude and idea for the drive. She suggested that we would treat this return journey like a vacation every day as we completed the drive home. And so we did! We found interesting locations, towns, and restaurants for our meals. We enjoyed the various cuisines, people, and locales. We also read a lot of menus and signage for tourists everywhere we stopped.

This story gives the saying, "The road to recovery is very long," a deeper and more literal meaning for me. It was over 2,000 miles long!

Now and Then

It has been over two decades since I was busy everyday attending to responsibilities related to the education and schooling of young folks. I seemed to be absorbed, challenged, and busy then. These days I feel the same, that is, busy, absorbed, and challenged, but with a different focus. The differences are varied and many between "then and now." Back then, I was thinking about other folks' challenges and best-hoped-for outcomes. Now, I think of my family and personal challenges and best-hoped-for outcomes, not that I have anything of a serious personal nature to focus on. I feel blessed, every day.

My thoughts float like clouds in a clear blue sky above me. My thoughts are of my dearest companion, friend, and the love of my life. What shall we do for tonight, dine at home or at the Little? Shall we ride together or drive separately to the gym? What would you like to do this evening, read or watch a documentary? When can we plan for the time to go to see our great-grandbaby? When do we clear the garden and get it ready for spring planting? You know, the serious decisions we have to make while other friends are dealing with major significant life-changing ones. Indeed how blessed we are!

Back then, I was thinking about other folks' challenges and best-hoped-for outcomes. So it seems, in reality and in the present, nothing much has changed except, time. We are grateful for all that we have and the time to enjoy those pleasures of life we hold dear to our hearts. It seems one of the differences between the "then and now" was a paycheck. Perhaps? The "now" paycheck is valued in smiles, hugs, love, and time. Time together, time with family, time with friends. The never-ending love and the gift of time. What greater rewards are there? I can't think of any. I have, we have, much more than so many others have. We are blessed.

The Old Country Doctor

The year was 1980, and I had just been appointed as the new high school principal in the Parishville-Hopkinton Central School District. The following year, I was selected and hired as the superintendent of the district. Small schools usually appoint on a year-to-year basis a local medical doctor to serve on a retainer as the district's physician. The services required may include conducting physicals for students on sports teams, completing the state-required annual bus drivers' physicals, and other emergency and student health related services. Parishville had one local physician, Dr. Max Thaler, whose home office was located in the town. Dr. Thaler was well known and loved by everyone in the community as well as the surrounding towns. In addition, he was affiliated with the Potsdam Hospital where he cared for his patients that required hospitalization and where he delivered all the babies of the greater community.

After my appointment as superintendent, our family moved to Parishville, where we built a new home. Our son Todd attended the local school, and we became participating members of the community. During our third year of living in Parishville, Todd became very sick. It began with a long-lasting headache, a fever, sore throat, difficulty swallowing, and total exhaustion. As parents, naturally we became very concerned and worried. We wished for Todd to be seen by one of the doctors in Rochester, where we and Todd had been patients before we moved. Our other choices of where to turn were limited. We could take him to the hospital in nearby Potsdam, the hospital in Watertown almost two hours away, or drive four hours to Rochester. Our most reluctant choice was to take him to the local physician, Dr. Thaler. We decided to have him seen by Dr. Thaler first and then on the weekend drive to Rochester for him to see a doctor we knew personally for a follow-up and second opinion.

We called Dr. Thaler's office late in the afternoon when we arrived home after work and realized Todd had not improved after a day of bed rest but was still very sick with a high temperature. We called the office number and described Todd's symptoms. The nurse asked us to bring him right away even though it was now approaching the dinner hour, and the office had closed. We drove to the doc's home/office and parked on the street in front. The home, best described as modest, had a short sidewalk from the street to the step of the front porch. We walked to the porch, proceeded to the door, and turned the antique hand cranked doorbell located in the center. Dr. Thaler's nurse greeted us in what was clearly German-influenced English, offered us seats in the waiting room, and told us she would summon the doctor. We smelled the aroma of cooked food coming from the kitchen as we looked around the waiting room, which appeared to be either the family room or perhaps a leisure reading room. The bookcases were loaded with dozens of old and new books, magazines and journals, many of which appeared to be medical in nature as indicated by their titles. The bookshelves were all slightly bowed near the middle due to the heavy weight of their contents. The furniture was comfortable but well used. It was evident to us that this room in particular had not been dusted or tidied up for some period of time. The top of the bookcases held apparatus of a medical and scientific variety, including lab glassware, titration tubes and stands, a very old brass microscope, various boxes, and medical models.

The nurse invited the three of us into the adjoining examination room, complete with an old adjustable wooden examination table with leather padding and on top of that white paper. We were introduced to Dr. Thaler by his nurse, and she excused herself to what I presumed to be the kitchen. The doctor asked Todd to strip down to his underwear and be seated on the table. A 13-year-old is a bit reluctant to remove all his clothes in front of Mom and Dad, but he did as requested. No examining gown was offered. This was simply getting down to business. After asking all the questions about symptoms and what brought us in, Dr. Thaler proceeded to examine Todd with his stethoscope and then placed a parabolic mirror (the shiny one with a small hole in the middle) on his head and asked Todd to "open wide," while he examined his throat, and tonsils. Next he poked, prodded, and thumped, various parts of his neck, armpits, chest, and other parts of his body. He sat and appeared to be deep in thought for just a moment and then told us he was going to take some blood samples, which he did.

He turned to all three of us and told us he was convinced that Todd had mononucleosis, or mono, and it was very contagious. He shared with us that Todd had swollen lymph nodes and tonsils and that he wished to monitor his liver function and spleen, hence the reason for the blood draw. He said he would call us at home as soon as he had the lab test results. He further told us to keep him home and not allow him to go to school or interact with any of his friends.

"Keep him in bed, feed him soup, and have him drink plenty of fluids. For his aches and pain, give him acetaminophen or ibuprofen. As parents, keep all your food and dishes separate from Todd's, wash your hands as often as you can, and be very careful with tissues, hankies, sneezing, and coughs. Keep him in bed!"

We asked "How long does this mono last?" Dr. Thaler told us, "At least two weeks and perhaps as long as a month." So here we were, and both Mom and Dad work. What were we to do? Dr. Thaler told us, he must stay in bed and rest, not go to school. If he wants to watch TV or read, he'll be fine. We were to consider this a vacation from school for Todd.

Dr. Thaler called us at home later that evening to see how Todd was feeling and said he wanted to monitor him and do another blood draw in a week. His nurse would set up the appointment for us. Charlotte and I did not have a lot of confidence in the advice and the office visit. We decided to call our family doctor in Rochester the next day. Our Rochester doctor patiently listed to our concerns and asked us if he could speak with Dr. Thaler on our and Todd's behalf. We agreed. Our doctor called us back the following day and relayed that he had spoken with Dr. Thaler, and he agreed with the diagnosis, the blood draw, the need to monitor — everything we were told. In his opinion, there was no need for us to bring Todd to Rochester for further examination. We were a bit embarrassed because of our lack of trust and confidence in our own "country doctor."

Todd was back in school in three weeks. Dr. Thaler made house calls several times checking on him before giving his final OK to return to school but limited his activities for several more weeks.

During the house calls, we shared tea and chats and so became friends. My mother and grandmother were planning a visit to see us and to stay for a few days. We decided to invite Dr. Thaler and his wife to join us for dinner one evening while they were there. Mom and Grandma were most positive about our planned evening together, and so a date was set.

I did not know all these details before our evening together. Dr. Max Thaler, and his nurse and wife, Angela, were survivors of World War II. Max was born in 1909. My mom was born in 1916, and my grandmother was born in 1895. Over many dinners, evenings together, and conversations, we were to learn that Max was born in Magierow, Poland, of poor Jewish parents. He completed his medical training at the University of Vienna, Austria, where he met and married Angela. When the war erupted, Max and Angela fled to Switzerland (a neutral country) to escape persecution. While in Switzerland, Max served as physician in a refugee camp. In 1948 Max and his family moved to

New York City to join Angela's parents, who had immigrated before the war. During the next two years, Max completed his residency requirements and became licensed to practice medicine in New York State. Then in 1950, after answering an ad in a medical magazine, he opened a family practice in Parishville and became connected with Potsdam Hospital.

During dinner that first evening, table talk included a discussion of how much our four seniors enjoyed playing Scrabble, so naturally the evening concluded with an intense and serious game. Charlotte and I soon realized the four of them were in a much different and advanced league of word knowledge and ability than we were. We were simply happy to watch and enjoy the conversations and keep them supplied with hot tea and a sweet now and then. There were many dinners together with the Thalers when Mom and Gram came north to visit us. Max and Angela were always eager to join us for dinner and never tired of the visitations, conversations, and Scrabble.

Dr. Thaler remains, in my mind, the very definition of an old country doctor. He continued to live and serve the community after we had moved to another part of the state. He worked and lived in Parishville until his retirement and passed away in his beloved hospital in Potsdam. The story of his life and service as well as his medical bag are on display in the Potsdam Historical Society.

SAVE THE RECEIPT

Who buys a light bulb that is guaranteed to last for 13.7 years, and where do you keep the receipt in case it only lasts for 12.5 years? Why would one even think or worry about these questions when you are eighty-two years old? Darned if I know, but to even have this question enter into your conscience thought process is unsettling at my age, or perhaps any age?

I was in the bathroom, brushing my teeth, and it seemed to be a little dimmer than the last time I stood in that same spot. I looked up at the four glass fixtures over the mirror and noticed one bulb was not working. I mentioned this to my wife and to my amazement she had also noticed it. I thought about it for a moment and remembered the last time this happened I bought extra bulbs for "just in case" and thought they were downstairs in the closet.

My memory, for extra lightbulbs, hasn't dimmed. I wish I could say that about other more important things in my life and world. Sure enough, there was a box of four of them in the closet, all 40 watts and clear glass. And on the box, in my own hand, which I had forgotten about, was written, "Used but still good." Must be the old ones that I had replaced not so long ago.

Being a person with "old person's thinking," I thought to myself, I need to buy four more for the next time this happens. No, better yet, I need to buy eight more so I'll be all set for as long as we live in this house. I also remembered, since these bulbs are incandescent and are now phased out of production, eight replacements for the future is brilliant thinking on my part. Tomorrow I will plan on stopping at the electrical supply company to stock up.

The following morning I did go to the warehouse and took my old box of bulbs with me to show the clerk exactly what I was searching for.

"Good morning, how can I help you?"

"Do you happen to have any of these in stock?"

"I think we may, but I'll have to go upstairs to see if I can find them. Let me check the computer first. They are four inch, clear glass, 40 watt. Inventory indicates we have twenty seven. You do know they do not make these any more, and when they are gone, they are gone. We are just selling these for a good price just to get rid of them."

At this point, my brain shifts into high gear. Will I need four or should I buy eight? "Good price" certainly got my attention!

"How much are they?"

"They are $1.69 each."

"OK, I'll take eight of them."

"It will be a few minutes while I go upstairs to find them."

Several minutes pass.

"I brought the box down, there are twenty-seven here. You wanted eight, right? Let me get you a smaller box to put them in to take with you. You know you can get these in LEDs?"

"I don't like LEDs. I like the clear glass"

"The LEDs are clear glass! Come with me, I have a fixture of four over here to show you. You can't tell the difference."

"Oh, they look very nice. I like them. How much are they?"

"Walk back with me to the computer, and I'll look them up for you."

"The best ones are $7.69 each. But I also have the same clear glass ones in LEDs in 40 watt for $2.17."

"What's the difference?"

"Nothing really, just a different supplier."

"How long will they last?"

"I don't know. Let me get a box."

Once again, she disappears into the back supply room returning with a box of LED bulbs.

"It says right here on the box in large print, 'Guaranteed to last for 13.7 years.'"

"I'm sorry for all the trouble. Can you take back the incandescence ones and sell me four of the LEDs?"

"No problem."

On the drive home, I'm thinking, do I need to save the receipt, just in case? And if I should, where should I put it as I will never remember where I saved it?

PATIENCE

My friends tell me, "Age is just a number, it's how young you feel that matters." For them that may be true and in fact it is for me also, however young I feel on any particular day when I wake up. Each morning upon waking, I know I'm either a "young" or "old" 81. At both my "young" and "old" age, my patience shortens with every passing year. I notice my patience almost disappears when I stand in a long line even when I know at the end of it, a wonderful concert, play, movie, or dinner will be my reward. My patience evaporates when the younger me awoke this morning, and for some unknown reason, a friend decided to tell me about his latest medical appointment and the consult with his doc, the list of meds he is on, for how long he has to take them, and about all the side effects they will cause. This confession took place while a group of us were involved in a friendly neighborhood poker game. Why in the world does he think we have any interest in the scripts he is taking and why he needs to take them? Please, just deal the cards! We are here to play poker, not to listen to your pains, problems, and doc visitations. "Age is just a number; it's how young you feel that matters." No, I think it's more than just a number. It's how patient you feel that matters.

I have no patience for the long stories in *The New York Times*, just tell me in the first paragraph, what, where, why, when, and how old they were when they died. There I go again, forgetting all about,

"Age is just a number." Long lines of traffic test my patience especially when I've been driving on the interstate at 65 mph and now we've come to a complete halt and the guy behind me almost relocated my back bumper in the rear seat of my car. I have no patience for his or her lack of paying attention while driving. I notice lately that traffic lights, when they turn red, seem to stay on longer than they used to. Perhaps traffic lights have lost their patience also? I doubt that's the case, but I can't help but wonder if it's an age thing?

My mother always said, "Patience is a virtue." I've almost have totally lost my virtue, and it is blatantly obvious on the days when I do rash things. For example, when I burnt my mouth on a sip of hot tomato soup from a spoon instead of waiting for it to cool. I used to blow on the spoon to cool the soup, but that was before COVID entered our lives. It is the same with birthday cakes and candles with COVID around. You can't really blow out the candles without blowing all over the cake that will be cut into pieces that someone else is going to eat. Just the other day, on my morning drive to the gym, I had my McDonald's coffee in one hand while waiting for a break in traffic. I was impatient, took a sip, and burnt my tongue again. Same spot on my tongue again as from the hot tomato soup. That's another "thing" about being 81, I've graduated to becoming a "slow learner."

Tolstoy's take on this issue was, "The two most powerful warriors are patience and time." My assessment is, at the current moment, I'm very short on both. But then, there is no need for me to be a warrior as in days past when I fought long and hard for the down trodden and disadvantaged.

Gandhi's thoughts on this was, "To lose patience is to lose the battle." Well, I haven't lost yet, but I need reinforcements. I found a few. At our last poker game, one of the guys, when it was his time to deal, picked up the deck, held it tight in his hands, and proceeded to expound on his latest visit to his doctor's office accompanied by his lifelong history of medical problems, and the new prescribed meds he needed to take. It was at the point that an uncontrollable voice within me tickled my vocal cords and made me blurt out, "We're here to play cards. Deal the cards!" A choir of voices around the table joined in, "For ____ ____ ___ ____, deal the cards we don't want to hear about your medical problems!" I found my reinforcements at that poker game and powerful warriors they were. Of course, these brother warriors are also older like myself. I didn't think to ask them how young or old they were when they woke up that particular morning.

Joyce Meyer said, "Patience is not the ability to wait, but the ability to keep a good attitude while waiting." Ahh, that's it. Attitude. That's what I need to work on, my attitude.

BUT I CAN STILL DANCE

Charlotte and I enjoy a group of friends we have known for many years. We refer to ourselves as the Gang of Eight, four couples that enjoy each other's company and often gather for an evening's activity or a dinner. We are bound together by our interest in or practice of eating (otherwise known as dining), golf, automobiles, travel, the historical society, gardening, theater, or just about any other excuse we may need to gather. This brings us to a New Year's Eve party that did not happen.

Traditionally, we gather each New Year's Eve at the country club for a dinner dance, to count down the Ball in Times Square, and to ring in the New Year. This year the country club decided to change it up a bit and offered a Christmas dinner dance in lieu of the regular New Year's Eve activity. As soon as the word was out, the Gang of Eight was all in on this new venture.

It turned out to be a great evening with an outlandish as well as a delicious buffet, beginning with hors d'oeuvres and ending with a wide variety of desserts. The music began soon after we were seated, and we were ready to dine. After many rounds of libations from the bar which put everyone in the perfect party mode and mindset, dancing commenced. Everyone was on the dance floor most of the evening. The music theme was straight out of the 1950s and included many of our groups' favorites. As you've already figured out, the Gang of Eight may be a bit older than the average population but not old enough apparently to draw undue attention to ourselves on the dance floor. No sooner had we finished dining than everyone was up and acting like it was our high school prom night. We danced and danced some more, well into the evening for hours to the tunes of our youth and such favorites as: "Tutti Frutti," "Great Balls of Fire," "Rock Around the Clock," "Be-Bop-A-Lula," "Who Do You Love?," "That'll Be The Day," "You Send Me," "Cheek To Cheek," "Fever," and "All I Have To Do Is Dream."

Can you imagine a gaggle of 70- and 80-year-olds acting like high school seniors on the dance floor? Well, I can because I was there. But I was also thinking at the time, that a lot of these folks are going have trouble getting out of bed in the morning and probably will be sore all the next day. I guess there was just the right number of bottles of wine at our table along with the cocktails to provide lubrication for the joints, rid the body of muscle spasms, and relax the mind, as well as possibly throwing inhibitions out the window. It was a crazy fun time!

When I was on the dance floor and also back at our table catching my breath, I noticed a group of four women enjoying every dance as we had been. Yes, every dance without a break. One of these woman, in particular, seem to be having an outstanding time accompanied by the other three. I noticed how thin she was, not anorexic thin but thin enough to make me wonder. Her build was evident to me as her black slacks and silk blouse appeared as if they were perfectly designed to be hung on a mannequin in the women's department at Von Maur, complete with black high heels.

Toward the end of the evening I was standing near the dance floor waiting for Charlotte to return from the ladies room when this same woman walked over to me and said something I didn't quite understand because of the loud music and probably because my hearing is not the best in that kind of situation. Her large eyes were enhanced with perfectly applied make-up, but something seemed missing. With the background noise, I was only able to pick out a couple of words she spoke to me, one of which sounded like "dance." Now I wasn't sure if she was talking about the last dance or commenting on all the dancing we were doing that evening or asking me to dance with her. I was a bit embarrassed as I did not understand what she was trying to communicate to me. What I said in response did not make any more sense from what I thought she had said to me, and my embarrassment continued.

"Yes, I love this music and I'm having a good time. I'm just waiting for my wife to return to the table, and I think we'll dance a few more if we can find the energy."

Again, she mentioned the word "dance" in response to my comment but I couldn't make out exactly what she was trying to say to me. I just made some kind of a jerk's reply.

"It's been a lovely evening. Charlotte and I have enjoyed our dinner and the music."

She looked at me quizzically, a bit surprised, and then she touched my soul through her eyes as she said, "You don't know me, do you?"

"No, I'm sorry I don't. I'm Gary, and my wife is Charlotte. Pleased to meet you."

She replied, " I can't drive anymore. I can't read my books, or write. I have trouble talking and remembering words and what to say. I have Alzheimer's, *but I can dance!*"

"Yes, you can! I was watching you dance. You are a fabulous dancer! I wish you a Merry Christmas!"

My eyes filled as I returned to my seat. My vision blurred as I looked at Charlotte and the other Gang of Eight members, and I repeated what I had just been told. One member of our group indicated that he would share with me her story the next time we were together as he knew her and her family well. My heart was full of appreciation for the season and the gifts I already had received. I am glad to say that young lady was still on the dance floor when of our Gang of Eight departed for home that evening.

A Fire-Breathing Dragon

We have an older home that turned out to be perfect for our grandchildren. By older, I mean circa 1850 with two floors and two separate stairways to the second floor which allows kids to circle around and between the floors without having to retrace their steps, up one set of stairs and down another. This feature turns out to be a great aid when playing hide and seek. To add to the fun of that game, we added a secret passage-way and an extra door in the rear of the kitchen broom closet that exits into a room off the living room, allowing one to choose yet another door and stairway to a second basement. The original basement has a door off the family room with its own set of stairs to allow access and egress to and from it.

When re-doing the home the first time, we returned all the floors to their original constructed format, that is, Canadian white pine boards, ten-plus inches wide and one and a half inches thick. The floor in the dining room, just in front of the front porch door, was missing a knot which fell out eons ago. We always kept a small carpet on the floor just in front of that door to cover the missing knot hole as well as a place to keep your shoes when entering from out of doors. When our grandchildren were very young, we would pull the carpet back so the grand babies could get down on their hands and knees and put their eye right up to the knot hole and peek down into the basement. With every grandchild's visit, the first thing they did when arriving was to run over to the front door, pull the carpet away, and look down into the basement. I soon realized this was a pattern, so to make it more enchanting and exciting, I made a weekly diorama for their basement "peek-a-boo." This was accomplished by attaching a large black bucket to the bottom of the floor board, adding a light, and various objects; plastic or plaster animals, cars, figurines, dinosaurs, birds, jewels, or anything the little ones may be interested in. The setup changed every week, and with each visit to Grandma's house, the knot hole became the very first place for them to explore.

We believe the house had a summer kitchen added sometime in the mid-to-late 1800s. The summer kitchen area became our family room. The original summer kitchen had a large built-in pantry cupboard with several shelves complete with a set of doors from the floor to the top of the cabinet. We quickly converted the cabinet to what we called the toy cupboard for the grandchildren and filled it with games, cars, trucks, toys, children's books, balls and jacks, gyroscope, dominoes, and all other sorts of play things. It was usually the second place for the grandchildren to visit and explore after first checking out the knot hole in the floor.

I built a small 400-square-foot building on the back of our property to have as a hide-a-way to enjoy without being tempted by the TV or other technology and just for a place to read and enjoy the rain and snow storms off the lake. It was cozy, complete with a stove for warmth. We called it our Tea House, with the idea of having a cup of tea to enjoy while reading. It has morphed into a wine house to be honest as we tend to enjoy a glass of wine while reading our books as much as we enjoyed the hot tea. When I built the Tea House, I had our grandchildren in mind as I designed a large metal, sculptured dragon head and tail to be affixed to each end of the roof ridge pole. The dragon head was then electrified so its red eyes would glow in the dark of the evening hours and a key lock switch was wired to an electric ignition so the propane gas could be ignited and flames were able to roar out of its open mouth between its teeth and over its tongue. The fire breathing dragon became operational at the touch of a button! Our grandchildren were delighted with it as much as I was. Then the fun began with the set-up questions for little people visits, with no right answers. When young children and grandkids visited, I would ask:

Do you know about dragons?

Do you believe that dragons exist?

Do you know that dragons can breathe fire?

Would you like to see a dragon and see it breath fire?

It did not matter how they answered as I would lead them to realize they were about to witness a dragon breathing fire. Many doubting children came to believe in fire-breathing dragons while visiting the Tea House at Grandpa Buehler's!

THE BLACK HAND

The title does not refer to the lawless secret society that was engaged in criminal activities connected with organized crime. In the past, there was such an organized crime ring in our own hometown of Rochester, New York, known as The Black Hand Society, which was operational during the years of Prohibition. A book has been published recently detailing the operation of the society and the families and members of the organization involved. For the record, let me be clear, that I have never been a member of The Black Hand Society although I can relate to the title, explained in the following tale.

The tab on the hanging folder, in my old filing cabinet read, "B&P Contractors." The business card included in said file had the B&P logo on it, with two names printed across the top, one that started with *B* and the other with *P*, an address, two phone numbers, and across the bottom, the motto: "Protect and Increase Your Investment." This card was attached to a flyer which read:

Dear Homeowner:

This is to advise you that B&P Contractors are available for exterior painting and roofing. We are experienced, fully insured and dependable. Our company uses the finest paint and roofing materials. We consider our work to be of exceptional quality. B&P Contractors enjoy the position of being competitive price-wise, and would appreciate you contacting us to compare our costs.

Since we would appreciate your business, we will give FREE estimates. To arrange for a written estimate, please contact the undersigned.

Thank you for your consideration.
Gary Buehler xxx-xxxx / Bob Pedzich xxx-xxxx

Bob and I were fairly new to the teaching profession, and both of us were married. My wife and I had two daughters, and Bob and his wife were expecting their second child. As teachers, we both were facing a summer with no paychecks expected until after the new school year was to start and it would not be until mid-September when our cash flow would begin once more. To fill the income gap, we decided to do what many other teacher educators had done for years, paint houses. We went one step beyond, not only would we paint houses but also put new roofs on as well as build additions. B&P would survive and prove very profitable, but how did that very first job go?

Also in the file was the first signed contract which read:

Enclosed is the signed contract for the painting of our home.

When convenient, please call or stop by and we can finalize the color selection and the timing of your work. As we mentioned, our family will be on vacation the first two weeks in August.
I look forward to hearing from you.

David J. A__________

The letter was typed and on letterhead from an office in Rochester.

My confidence as a salesman was affirmed, but the letterhead was a bit unnerving as I thought to myself, *"Great, our first customer and our first contract is from an attorney no less. We've got two weeks to get it done perfectly, and our reputation for word-of-mouth recommendations is riding on this!"*

I immediately called Bob when I finished opening the mail and read the letter to him. His response was, "Well, we are off and running!"

The estimate and contract, in my own hand writing, read:

> *Scrape-Prime-Paint where necessary. Paint entire house, garage, and fence, in color selections and clean out gutters. Paint the fence.*

Upon arriving on the job site, I saw a house and garage that appeared much larger than I remembered when I was first there to write the estimate. The fence around the pool seemed to go on and on forever, a much larger rectangle than I remembered it being. What was I thinking?

Since my business partner, Bob, was afraid of heights and I wasn't that enthralled about being too far off the ground either, we had recruited another teacher friend, by the name of Lee, who was a volunteer fireman and had no fear of heights. Neither Bob nor I inquired of him if he liked to paint or was good at it. We just wanted to know if heights bothered him. Turns out he had no fear of heights but hated painting, was not good at it, and got more paint on himself and the roof shingles than on the siding.

Note to self: have a complete interview before offering employment to anyone and be sure to measure total length of fence as well as noting detail of design.

Starting on a Monday, three of us were working on the house and garage, and one of our crew was assigned to wire brush, scrape, and then paint the wrought iron fence that surrounded the pool. By Thursday of that first week, we finished the painting and trimming of the house and garage but not the fence. It was clear that it would take several more days for one person to finish the fence at the current pace. I told the guys that during our half hour lunch break I was leaving to get materials for the fence, and I would finish painting it that afternoon! I also told the crew I'd grab sodas on the way back for everyone and took orders. I went to the closest auto parts store I could find and returned back to the job site with refreshments and my painting equipment.

After lunch, I asked the guys to spread out all the drip cloths we had with us and place them under the unpainted portions of the fence and once that was done, to get up on the roof and clean up all the paint drops on the shingles that were next to the dormers. I returned to the pool fence, slipped on the wool car wash mitt, dipped it into the gallon of paint, squeezed hard to get rid of excess and then put my fingers around each iron part of the fence and ran it up, down, and around the scroll work of each section. It worked like a charm! I finished "painting" the fence that afternoon. The drop cloths were folded up with all the paint on them. As they couldn't be salvaged, they were tossed in the back of my car and destined for the trash cans at home. The job was completed at the end of the first week, and we moved on to the next house we were contracted to paint the following Monday.

While my painting method worked, I had an ugly black hand for a while, especially around all my finger nails and the folds of skin on my knuckles where paint thinner and scrubbing were utterly ineffective, thus bringing us back to the title of this tale.

WHAT IS *THAT* SMELL?

We had just moved into our first new home that we could barely afford. In fact, before our mortgage was approved, we had tried to purchase a smaller starter home in the city, but due to my total annual earnings, I did not qualify for that mortgage. In order to qualify, I had to increase my annual income. So I applied for and was successful in securing a second job. I had mechanical skills and some automobile repair knowledge, so I was hired at a service station to perform car care and maintenance. I assumed that I would be doing automobile engine tune ups and an occasional oil and filter change. But in reality it turned out to be steady stream of filling gas tanks and oil changes. After two weeks, I resigned the position because I was extremely frustrated, spending most of my time doing oil and filter changes and no engine tune-ups. My short tenure at the new job was now completed, and I did not have any more engine oil running down my neck, dripping into my hair, on my hat, and no more dirty and oily clothes smelling like high-test gasoline.

Although we did not qualify financially to buy an older home, it did not deter us from driving around on weekends looking at houses. During one of these Sunday drives, we found ourselves in a new development housing track. After some discussion with a sales person and reading the advertisements, we were led to believe that we could qualify for a mortgage on a new home here fairly easily with our annual income. We could not even begin to understand what was happening. We did not qualify financially to purchase a small starter home, but somehow we could be eligible for a new home, which was several thousand dollars more than the older, smaller home. At that time, it was the norm for the mortgage business and banking.

We almost qualified for the bank's approval on the new Domus Builder's home in this particular track, but not quite. After additional discussion with the bank's loan officer, I had a plan. I would secure another part time job and then, with the additional income added to my annual salary, I would be able to reapply and thus qualify for the mortgage. I contacted a family acquaintance and friend who was the owner of a construction company, and I was successful in obtaining a position in the company in the garage, working on the trucks and heavy equipment. It worked out perfectly and this did the trick. My mortgage application was approved, and we moved into our new home in suburbia.

Having no money left over after all the required closing costs, we had to severely compromise and cut a lot of corners to reduce expenses. For us, cutting corners meant no blacktop driveway, just gravel, skipping the needed storm and screen windows, no family room addition, and a variety of other options that we could not choose. Like most of our neighbors, we did not have a lawn but instead just a rough graded lot. Soon we were busily picking up stones both large and small, raking dirt to make a smoother lot, and planting inexpensive fast-growing rye grass seed. Most of our new neighbors were also fertilizing and watering their new lawns hoping to soon seen blades of green grass poking through the bare and brown soil. Many of the new lawns had straw covering the soil as an aid to conserve the watering of the new grass seed and to aid in its germination and sprouting.

Thinking outside of the box, I borrowed a trailer and headed to my aunt and uncle's farm several miles south of where we were located. When I arrived, I asked my Uncle George if he had some aged manure I could have. He suggested a specific pile in the barnyard that was a few years old and was, as he referred to it, "ripe" and would be perfect for my application. Lucky me I thought, as this pile also included bedding. Just so we are all on the same page, farmers spread straw in the areas where the livestock are housed to assist in keeping the area clean and to make it more comfortable for the animals to lie down. So there it was, a gift for me and it did not cost me a penny — ripe manure complete with straw, all in one load. One trip and free! I needed this, or so I thought.

When I arrived back home I thought I was Farmer Brown. I literally backed the trailer up on the front lawn and proceeded to take pitch fork and began spreading the load of manure all over the newly planted grass seed. It was a big load so I had enough to do the side yard and the back yard as well. A few of my neighbors were interested in what I was doing, but I admit they were more curious as to the "why" of it all. A few offered an opinion that they hoped it would work. Work it did! Following is the tale of how well it succeeded.

We had two girls at this time, the youngest was just starting kindergarten. When we attended the school's Open House and visited with each one of the teachers, the Art teacher shared with us, among other things, that our daughter is somewhat stubborn and inflexible. This indeed took both of us by total surprise as we thought she was very quiet, shy, and soft-spoken. Naturally we wished to know how the teacher had arrived at her opinion and conclusion. She shared the experience she had during the class art lesson. She had instructed all the students to draw and color the house where they lived. Our daughter drew a picture of our house on the paper and colored it as instructed to do so. The students' drawings were posted around the room. Our daughter's drawing revealed that indeed the lawn was brown. As further discussion ensued, we understood that the teacher's instructions were, "Tammy, grass is green, not brown. You need to color it green." Tammy's reply was, "Not mine, mine's brown!" Tammy had refused to color it green instead of brown.

We watered and watered our so-called lawn. The rye grass began sprouting and after some time, the thin green blades began appearing above the manure that was mixed with the old straw. Then a funny thing happened on the way to becoming a full-fledged lawn. Other things began to appear, and we wondered what those strange weeds were? Some were serious weeds, as in thistles. Others appeared to be corn along with sprouting wheat and oats. The unintended consequences of being Farmer Brown! Then it began to rain for a bit. The sun came out, but the wind blew too, and the barnyard aroma began a serious emergence. Friendly neighbors were suddenly becoming less friendly along with comments like, "What is *that* smell?"

One neighbors to the east of us took particular pride in their lawn and invested a tremendous amount of time, and I would expect money, to have the perfect lawn. In the meantime, Farmer Brown was incubating a tremendous and serious batch of dandelions. When they reached full maturity, the wind, as it did the majority of the time, continued to blow from the west to the east and managed to seed the neighbor's lawn with the same fine crop of dandelions that we had raised.

One thing about a rotary mower, it works well when one has to mow down weeds, or corn, wheat, and oats. After mowing, green is green, especially when one drives by to observe, at twenty miles an hour and takes a glance. But on closer inspection, one realizes something is not quite right. Be advised not to take it up with Farmer Brown, as he's very defensive and apologetic. But the good news is, the aroma has finally dissipated, and no one asks anymore, "What is *that* smell?"

It Was a Different Time

The family had grown to five. Mom was in graduate school at Alfred University; Dad was well into his career in education. There had been a few lean years which resulted in many — let's say, cheap, and leave it at that — worn-out old cars in the driveway. There had not been a new one purchased for the family for fifteen years. The older cars were never a challenge as Dad was able to fix just about anything and keep them serviceable, reliable, and on the road. The only downside in this arrangement was the embarrassment it brought to the family members for always having "junkers" to drive, and having two of them parked in the driveway. The neighbors, with their new shiny station wagons, never seemed to mind or say anything dismissive when the annual bonus from a major local employer was announced, and it was new car shopping time for them once again.

Finally, it was determined that it was time to treat the family to a new chariot as financial stability had been fairly established. Mind you, not just any chariot would satisfy the need after years of sacrifice. No sir, it was time for a special vehicle. And so it came to be, a brand new Chrysler four-door sedan was ordered from the dealer.

The family had made plans to travel for five weeks of vacation during the summer to enjoy the wonders, sights, and sounds of the Old West. The big sedan allowed plenty of room for the three kids in the back seat, or so Mom and Dad thought. Three abreast would include the eldest daughter, a senior in high school, her younger sister, a freshman, and their "baby" brother, who was nine years old. With two teen-aged older sisters, the "boundary line" drawn by the young prince on the rear seat seemed to be crossed at the most inopportune times resulting in a test of serenity as well as patience for both parents as well as his older sisters.

The year was 1978, and CB radios were very popular among truckers, wannabe truckers, and even the general public. Yes, that big shiny black Chrysler was equipped for the cross-country trip with a factory ordered and installed CB radio! The CB was to be used to check on traffic patterns, road conditions, speed traps, and as a last resort, for family entertainment to avoid boredom for the passengers on the long journey on the Interstates.

Every trucker and CB operator has a name or *handle*. The family chariot was christened *Mariah,* from the then-popular song which gave the wind a name. Five weeks were planned to visit national parks, Native American sites, and to experience the Old West. We planned to get west of the Mississippi River as soon as we were able, then to slow down, savor the Western states, and parks, and try to follow old Route 66 as much as possible. Interstate 40 runs close to Route 66 and parallel for much of the way, and it was our planned highway of choice.

It just so happened that on one of those full days of driving on I-40 we sort of played Tag with the same 18-wheel semi tractor-trailer truck most all of one morning. We seemed to select the same rest stops for potty breaks or snacks or lunch as that semi. The young one in the back seat noticed the truck we were traveling with, and mom and dad allowed him to spend time on the CB radio chatting with the driver, thereby avoiding some of the boundary issue violations that inadvertently were occurring on the rear seat. No one complained that he was chatting on the CB radio as he was occupied and not bothering his older sisters. It all started innocently enough with the little guy, microphone in his hand, and chatting on the radio.

"Breaker, breaker, this is *Mariah*. You copy?"

"10-4 *Mariah*!"

"What's your handle?"

"*Hussle 2,* 10-4. Where you headed?"

"We're trucking over to Cal-i-forn-i-a, 10-4."

"*Mariah*, you following me to CA?"

"No."

"Where are you headed?"

"From Amarillo, Texas, this morning and maybe tonight, Albuquerque, New Mexico?"

"You sound pretty young to be out here freewheeling! You driving that black Chrysler?"

"No, that's my dad. He lets me use the CB."

"Tell you what, I've been seeing you behind me all morning and at the rest areas where we stop. Have you ever ridden in an 18-wheeler?"

"No."

"Would you like to?"

"YES!"

"Well, tell you what, I'm stopping in about 20 miles at the next rest area, and you can ride in the truck for a ways, and your parents and sisters can follow me in the car. You can be on the CB and talk to them all the time while we are running up the road."

"OK!"

"You and your parents talk, and we'll talk in person next stop to see what they think. 10-4."

As parents we didn't know quite what to think. Todd begged us to talk with the driver. His sisters were not supportive one iota. The next 20 miles went by very quickly. We pulled off into the car parking area at the rest stop, and the big rig pulled up opposite from us on the roadway. We piled out of the car, and the driver waved and walked over. There was a long conversation, and the offer was to have the young one ride in the tractor-trailer for the next 100 miles to a truck stop in Tucumcari, New Mexico. Young Todd would have the mic and be on the CB talking with us the entire time. The driver took all of us over to his truck to show it to us. We agreed to the offer and thought it would make a great experience and lasting memory of our trip and vacation, especially for the young guy.

Off they went and we followed behind noting license number, truck and trailer colors, name of the trucking company, etc. Todd was on the CB the entire time, describing how the gears are shifted, how the seat adjusts, the interior, gauges, lights, horn, and every detail in the cab. Mom and Dad were a bit worried about this needless experience and adventure, but nowhere close to the concerns his older sisters had. In fact, it was very quiet in the back seat the entire 100 miles.

The tale ends almost 45 years later when we find Todd with a commercial driver's license to operate a tractor-trailer making a career working and managing a diesel truck and equipment repair facility.

I'm just wondering what decision would you have made if you were the parents in that car?

Write your answer on the next page . . . :>)

One Way To Get To Your B&B

As we were enjoying the Scottish Highlands and staying for five days in the capital city of Inverness, we had the opportunity to explore Loch Ness and the many miles of its shoreline. We also were able to visit castles, take in the beauty of the area, visit the Culloden battlefield, and other areas of historical interest.

This trip required that I must attempt to try to master driving on the left-hand side of the road while seated in the driver's seat on the right-hand side of the vehicle. In addition, I had to master going left when entering and exiting with traffic in the "roundabouts." To add to the challenge of driving on the left, we had to find and exit on either the "third, fourth or fifth exit" to remain on route and to follow Apple's MapQuest verbal and visual directions on my phone. The timid of heart or nervous driver would find this exercise taxing and unsettling; I assure you. One thing we did not master apparently were the "one way" street signs or lack thereof. It happened this way one evening after having dinner at a downtown cafe. Of course a bit of alcohol was involved, as in just one glass of wine, but one always must be aware and careful.

Our evenings were highlighted by exploring and finding interesting places to dine. All found gems were within walking distances and included crossing the River Ness on the suspended foot bridge which not only swayed back and forth but also undulated up and down with every step taken. The journey home via the bridge adds to the lasting wine experience that accompanies a wonderful meal. One evening we selected a cafe in downtown Inverness that we decided was a bit too far from our B&B to walk, so we reluctantly elected to drive our rental car into the city and associated busy traffic. Without incident, we found a public parking lot, figured out the puzzle of paying in advance by using Scottish sterling pound coins, and received our reward of a paper ticket to be placed on our dashboard.

A short walk rewarded us with a comfy table, reserved in advance, and a menu of Scottish cuisine selections to choose from. If you haven't had the pleasure of enjoying a complete traditional Scottish, Irish, or English meal, I think you will find Scottish dining delightful, especially if your selection happens to be fresh seafood. Scallops are served fresh and complete, unlike scallops anywhere else I have ever experienced. At the end of the evening, we walked slowly back, retracing our steps, to find the car park. We exited the lot turning left, the direction we had driven down the street to find it when we had arrived earlier that evening.

I had only driven a short distance upon exiting the lot when I noticed a car that had turned off the main street traveling towards me with its headlights on. This was a typical narrow street in the UK which does not allow two cars to pass each other without one of the vehicles pulling over allowing the other to pass. I stopped in the middle of the street, trying to figure out where I was going to find a place to pull over and noticed the approaching car was not slowing down or pulling over to allow us to pass, but was continuing towards me at its same initial rate of velocity. Additionally, the vehicle's headlights were flashing, and the red and blue lights across the roof were now turned on. The car pulled up close to my front bumper and stopped. I thought about that glass of wine I had consumed with dinner. I looked at Charlotte and said, "What did I do wrong?"

Both officers exited the vehicle and arrived at my window on the driver's side as I lowered it.

"You are not from around here, are you?"

I thought for a just a moment and in my typical fashion replied, "How could you tell?"

"Well, for one thing, you are going the wrong way on a one-way street. Can you reverse this thing?"

I must have had the puzzled look on my face I always have when I don't know what just happened or don't understand the situation.

"How are you at backing up?"

Now I understood the reference to "reverse this thing."

"Not that good, but I have a back-up camera, and I can back up OK, I think."

"OK, reverse back to that exit of the car park, then turn right on St. John Ave., go to the third exit of the roundabout, stay on Fairfield Road until you come to the roundabout, and exit on A-83."

At this point, my eyes must have started to glaze over as I know I am not good at directions, and perhaps, just perhaps, my eyes started to cross. In any event, I was rescued.

"I know why you turned the wrong way on this street, you just wanted to meet two Bobbies. Right? Where are you going?"

"To our B&B."

"And where is your B&B?"

"Charlotte, where is our B&B? Oh, I have the address on the paper in my pocket."

Digging out the folded paper from my shirt pocket from under the seat belt, I replied, "We are staying at the Lyndon Guest House on 50 Telford Street."

Both officers conferred with each other for a moment, and then responded.

"We know where you are staying. Reverse to that first exit in the lot. We are going to pull forward and turn onto that street right there. Then you pull up behind us and just follow us, and we'll take you to your B&B."

"Thank you, officers!"

We did as instructed and followed them through the city for what I'd guess were four miles or so, right up to the driveway of our B&B. At this point in the parade, the Bobbies turned on all their flashing red and blue lights and touched the siren just to let the B&B owner and other guests as well as all the neighbors know the Yanks were found, rescued, and returned home safe and sound.

26
The Best Plans

We tried cramming ten pounds of adventure into a five-pound box on our recent excursion to the Netherlands and the United Kingdom, and I think we may have succeeded. In addition to spending several days in the cities of Amsterdam, London, Edinburgh, Inverness, Kirkwall, and Glasgow, we enjoyed Charlotte's special interest stopovers and places to visit. I must confess, I enjoyed them also as much as she did even if I was a bit unenthusiastic, though supportive, during the planning phase of our adventure. Now I'm a cheerleader and, no doubt about it, a slow learner.

A few years ago, Charlotte enticed me to watch with her, the Masterpiece Classic anthology, *Downton Abbey,* which is about the lives of the Crawley family and their household staff in the post-Edwardian era. I quickly became intrigued and interested in the episodes and I guess, a fan. We also enjoyed the most recent film, *Downton Abbey: A New Era.* All six TV seasons and the two films were recorded at and within the Highclere Castle which is in Hampshire, England. It was Charlotte's wish on our most recent trip to visit Highclere, and I must admit I was delighted as well after I "got with the program."

Another TV series we enjoyed watching together was *Doc Martin* which was recorded in a small remote town on the most

Western coast of England at Port Isaac. We made plans and arrangements to visit and stay in Port Isaac in the schoolhouse. The old school building is featured in several episodes. Since the series concluded, it has been converted to a hotel, and we were fortunate to be able to reserve a room and dinner for a few days. The downside of our visit is that both of us came down with COVID during this part of our adventure. Since the tourist season has not yet begun, we stayed safe and kept others safe by isolating in our room and venturing outside only when others were not around.

Another one of Charlotte's interests is reading, and one of her favorite authors is Jane Austen, and of course her novel, *Pride and Prejudice*. As an unanticipated and unplanned stop, we managed to make a few adjustments to our travel schedule and spend a day in the village of Chawton, where Jane Austen's house/cottage and museum is located. It is in a 17th century building that remains much the same as when Jane lived and wrote her novels there. Her writing desk and many other personal belongings are intact and able to be viewed up close and personal. Charlotte and I were delighted to be able to spend several hours visiting the village and the museum.

As for me, the bonus of our visit to Highclere Castle, where *Downton Abbey* was filmed, was that on the day of our visit, we were greeted by the owner of the estate and had the opportunity to listen to him for an hour as a part of the introduction and orientation session before our tour began. The owner is George Herbert, 8th Earl of Carnarvon, married to Fiona, 8th Countess of Carnarvon. The owner and his family reside at the castle and are committed to preserving it as well as the estate. No doubt the costs of maintaining, repairing, improving and restoring the castle and the estate are staggering. I would imagine funds are accrued from the filming and TV production rights as well as products sold as it is a producing farm estate. Actually, one interesting note is that Queen Elizabeth's horses were fed oats that were grown on some of the 1,060 acres.

The castle has more than 200 rooms. We toured many of the main areas that are shown in the films and TV series. We did see the secret door concealed in the library among the bookcases and when opened we walked through the doorway to the adjoining game room. For me, the visit was a glimpse back into history of one of the last aristocratic-owned farming estates in England as well as making a personal connection to the film and TV stage/set of *Downton Abbey*.

We changed some of our travel plans to allow us to visit these three unique places in England, and we are glad we did. As the saying goes from "To a Mouse," by Robert Burns: "The best-laid plans of mice and men often go awry." In our case when the plans went awry, the results were wonderful.

70 is a Long, Long Road

On a recent cross-country driving trip to Arizona, we planned our evening's stay each morning by calling ahead and making reservations that same day. Our goal was to try to drive about 400 miles or so and then find a city on the map at about that distance from our starting point, search for our favorite hotel chain, and then call and make reservations for the evening. One key concern was how far the hotel was located from Interstate 70 as we did not want to drive too far from the exit to reach the hotel. On this blessed day, we called for reservations and the following unfolded:

Hotel: Hello, Holiday Inn Express.

Buehlers: Is this the front desk?

Hotel: Yes.

Buehlers: We would like to make reservations. Can you help us with that?

Hotel: Yes.

Buehlers: How far are you from Interstate 70?

Hotel: Where are you on 70?

Buehlers: We would like to know how far your hotel is located from the Interstate?

Hotel: Well, 70 is a long, long road. Where are you on 70? What city are you near?

Buehlers:	We would like to know how close you are located to the Interstate. How close are you to the exit?
Hotel:	What exit are you near?
Buehlers:	No, we would like to know how close *you* are to the exit.
Hotel:	Which exit are you at?
Buehlers:	No, how far is the Interstate from your hotel? How far is your hotel to the entrance of Interstate 70?
Hotel:	Oh, we are very close to the entrance of 70. It is just up the road.
Buehlers:	Great! We would like to make reservations for two for tonight.
Hotel:	I'm sorry, we are all filled up tonight and do not have any rooms left.

For this call, as usual, we had our phone on speaker. Charlotte and I just looked at each other, then rolled our eyes, and burst out in loud laughter, continuing to enjoy the ridiculous conversation we had just had, as both parties on the line were mis-communicating.

Gary: Now that was funny. Why didn't we ask if he had any rooms for tonight when he said, "This the front desk"?

Charlotte: Why didn't he tell us he was all booked when we started to inquire about how far it was from the Interstate?

Gary: Because he just wanted to know where we were on 70.

Charlotte: His statement that "70 is a long, long road" was too funny. I hope we weren't too rude on speaker phone when we were laughing so hard.

Gary: It was funny. I think we were OK. Let's look at the map again and pick another city.

Charlotte: OK. But 70 is a long, long road!

WHERE ARE YOU GOING?

It seemed simple enough. After all this was the second train we were taking during our extended holiday in the Netherlands and the United Kingdom. For this part of our excursion, the plan was to drop our rental car off in the town of Exeter, England, and take the train to Edinburgh, Scotland. We had toured England from London to Port Isaac and back to Exeter, having driven some 500 miles. We were assured we had plenty of time to make the trip from our B&B to the train station, but as a cautionary measure we left three hours earlier than the suggested travel route required. It happened to be a Saturday, and as we got closer to Exeter, we noticed we were following traffic detours and becoming entangled in a massive traffic jam. We were not worried as we had built so much extra time and so believed we were fine.

We had been told the car rental agency, where we had to drop the car off, was fairly close to the train station, about a 15-minute taxi ride. We finally arrived at the rental agency, checked into the office, took care of all the paperwork of returning the car and noticed we still had a couple of hours to get to the train station. The agent asked us if we wished for him to call a taxi to take us to the station. We told him that would be wonderful. He did mention that it was Saturday and things were very busy on the weekend in this small town. The response from the taxi dispatcher was it would be an hour and a half before a cab would be available to pick us up. I asked if he could call the other cab companies for us. He obliged and the response was the same, an hour and a half at the very least. I then asked him to try calling an Uber for us. At this point, when the answer for wait time was the same, the agent explained that one gentleman owned and ran all the taxis and Ubers in town. Well that explained a lot but didn't help our situation.

Since I knew the train station was "close" I inquired about walking directions. We each had a huge suitcase and a backpack and bags with us as we were traveling for seven weeks. It was simply too far for us to walk with all the luggage we had with us. I noticed a young man had arrived while we were waiting and was in the office to pick up his rental car. I began a conversation with him and found out he was a local resident who needed a car for a week while his own car was in the repair shop. I explained our situation and asked him if he could possibly take us to the station. He agreed and I offered to reimburse him for his time and trouble. The car he rented was tiny by US standards. We had this challenge — two *huge* suitcases plus assorted other luggage. Only one of those suitcases would fit in the trunk. The other had to be forced into the back seat and have the seat belt attached to it. Why? Because the weight of it mimicked a person sitting on the seat, and the computer in the car wasn't going to let us leave until "that person" buckled up.

We arrived at the station and settled our financial agreement with the Good Samaritan fellow. I am sure we covered most of his rental fee for the week. We were both very pleased. We arrived at the station with just a few extra minutes to catch our breath prior to boarding time. We were relieved and decided a latte would be just the thing we needed to calm down and relax a bit. While sipping, we were reading the electronic boards for arrivals and departures, found our train listed, and noted the platform we needed to find in order to board. We also saw a woman looking for the same information. After polite greetings, she told us to follow her as she knew where that platform was and that we had to cross over to the other side of the tracks to get to it. With just a few minutes left before boarding time, all three of us took off together with Charlotte and I pulling and pushing the huge suitcases. We stood on the platform and noticed the train coming towards us from quite a distance away, and our new friend noted it was our train but a few minutes early.

The train arrived, our friend told us to follow her as she knew where we could store our luggage for our long trip (seven hours). We settled our luggage on the storage racks and proceeded to find our seats. Charlotte found her seat but someone was already in it.

"I'm sorry to bother you, but I think you are in my seat."

"Oh, I'm sorry. . . . No, I am in the right seat by the number on my ticket. There must be some mistake. We'll have to find the conductor."

"Where are you going?"

"We're going to Edinburgh."

"Well, this train is going to London!"

"Ohhh, we are on the wrong train!"

It was easy to unravel our mistake as the conductor assured us that the train we should have boarded was just 10 minutes behind the train we were on, and all we had to do was to get off at the next station and then board the train behind us. The conductor called ahead to the station, so they were ready for us when the train stopped and assisted us in getting on the right train and also helped us with all our luggage.

In debriefing, we realized that back at the Exeter station, our new friend and we were looking for the same platform but never once asked each other where we were going or which train we were taking. With a little extra help, finally knowing we were in the right train, we were able to relax the rest of that afternoon and evening and enjoy our long ride north to Edinburgh instead of east to London.

WHAT HAPPENS IN LAS VEGAS....

Coming home from school at 12 years old and walking down the cinder driveway on a warm spring day, I could hear through the open windows, "God Bless America," on the TV. It was coming from the afternoon "Kate Smith Show." This was her signature song and the opening of her daily program. There were three TV channels in Rochester at that time, and at midnight all broadcasting ended, replaced by a test pattern which lasted until the first morning programing began. It was on the same TV show that a piano player made his first guest appearance. Both my mother and grandmother would laugh and point out his extravagant costumes and the candelabra which always sat on the piano. The peak of his popularity ran from the 1950s to the 1970s, when he was the highest paid entertainer in the world.

Early on in his career he also appeared on TV's DuMont's "Cavalcade of Stars," "The Jackie Gleason Show, " and then on his own show, "The Liberace Show," which was the first syndicated program on television. My mother and grandma seemed to love how he created a spectacle both on and off stage and became known as "Mr. Showmanship." He was for sure a controversial figure. When he moved to Las Vegas, he began to expand his act and made it even more extravagant, with more costumes and a larger supporting cast, which became his hallmark. He wore large ornate piano shaped rings with gold and diamonds on his fingers and draped himself in long heavy fur capes. An elaborate candelabra on the piano was always a permanent prop as a part of his show.

I just assumed as he became more popular with concert-goers, that my mother and grandmother continued to be fans of his. The thought never occurred to me that perhaps they both were making sport of him and his mannerisms, for after all was said and done, his television show, within two years of debuting was more popular than either "Dragnet" or "I Love Lucy."

In the early 1980s I was in Las Vegas for a convention and noted Liberace was still performing his shows and concerts. I was out to dinner with Jim Young, one of my board members at the time, and he suggested that later that evening we take a ride out to Liberace's night club, Tivoli Gardens. How Jim knew about Tivoli Gardens and the connection to Liberace, I didn't know and didn't ask, I just agreed. We took a cab down the strip to what I thought was a night club, but in reality was a combination Italian restaurant and bar. As the taxi pulled into the parking lot, neon light lit the area in all colors of the rainbow and a sparkling Rolls Royce covered in tiny mirrors with Liberace's name painted in the same rainbow colors on its side was parked by the main entrance. We had arrived and were greeted by the cabbie's, "This is it gentlemen!"

Entering, I was floored by all the kitsch, glitz, and the ornate white and gold piano complete with the trademark candelabra. The piano sat on a raised platform at the end of the bar. We were greeted by the bartender requesting what our choice of drinks might be and ordered. We looked around and noticed there were very few patrons in the bar at this late hour. We chatted with the bartender mentioning our observation, and he replied that Liberace had just arrived from his show at the Hilton and was here for his late dinner as usual, and if we stayed around, he might play a bit before heading home as was his usual routine. I was never one to be shy and said to the bartender:

"Do you mean Liberace is *here* now?"

"Yes, he is in the dining room at the moment enjoying his dinner."

I glanced to where the bartender nodded towards the entrance to the dining room. The entrance was blocked off with two chrome stanchions with a red velvet rope hanging between each one. I could see the mirrored walls and multiple crystal chandeliers hanging from the ceiling, but I could not see anyone seated at the tables. It appeared completely empty from our vantage point.

Jim and I took our drinks in hand and moved further down the bar so we could get a better glimpse into the dining room. We wandered over toward the cordoned-off restaurant entrance, and I noticed two gentlemen seated at one of the tables. There was not one ounce of doubt in my mind, it was *HIM*! No question! I stopped and apparently was staring at the table when I noticed that he raised his arm and motioned for us to come in. Did I see what I thought I saw? Jim nudged me on my back and shoulder and we walked across from the bar and into the room and over to his table. His guest, who was seated and having dinner with him, stood up and left. Somewhat stunned, I now found us standing at his table.

"Mr. Liberace," I said, "my mother was a fan of yours for years. She watched you on television on all the early shows you were on and also your own show. I am pleased to meet you in person."

There may have been other words exchanged but I do not remember them, but I do remember that he cleared a place on the table, took his white linen napkin, spread it out and asked:

"What is your mother's name?"

"Emma."

He took out a pen and wrote on the napkin: "To Emma, With love, Liberace"

With that, he handed it to me. We exchanged a few words along with our thanks and wandered back to the bar.

"Jim, do you believe that?"

Back in Rochester, the following Sunday, after church, Charlotte and I and our children went to visit Mom and Grandma at their home.

"Mom, you are not going to believe what I brought back from Las Vegas for you!"

I handed her the napkin. She unfolded it, read it and then placed it on the kitchen table and said:

"You know, I never really liked Liberace, but thank you for thinking of me. How did you get this?"

How I Use My Old T-Shirts

Of late, I've been thinking, talking, and writing about age. Not just age as in birthdays in general, but my age. At eighty-plus, what else does one think about? I don't know, I've never been this old before, so I haven't thought much about it. It's not worried thinking mind you, just one of the themes that's been going through my mind lately. I sometimes think about the energy crisis, climate change, world health issues, use of plastics, food supplies, and a host of themes that never entered my mind when I was younger. Then there's the theme about Gold's Gym.

Yes, that Gold's Gym, you know the one that originated in Venice, California, where all the macho guys and gals from the gym, wearing muscle T-shirts or tank tops, do pull-ups and push-ups on the beach with bulging muscles, six-pack abs, and arms bigger than they ought to be. That's what I'm talking about. Almost everyone is wearing Gold's Gym clothing with their copyrighted logo on them that depicts a muscular male holding a barbell, with the bar bending slightly in the middle due to the heavy weights of each end of it.

You see, for quite some time I have been going to Gold's Gym. I have yet to buy one of those shirts with their logo on it, and besides, I only wear my old worn out T-shirts there, so I have no need for their logo shirt. Let's face it, I can't wear a muscle shirt because I have none and probably won't have any in the foreseeable future, at least none worth showing off.

I'm classified as a "senior" by both Gold's Gym and Silver Sneakers, and I am indebted to them because most of the cost of my membership is paid for by my health insurance company. Their reasoning, as best as I can understand it, is the membership benefits me as I continue to accumulate birthdays and will assist me in staying independent as I get older. And I would guess, save them coverage expenses if I stay healthy and mobile longer and out of the hospital or the old person's home. My general plan for the gym is, that at my age, my weekly activities should include 150 minutes of moderate aerobic activity that will assist me in strength conditioning, improving my balance, and flexibility. The key here, at least for me, is balance. Every visit I make to any medical facility or doctor's office commences with, "Have you fallen lately?" I want to respond, "Hell no, I go to Gold's Gym almost every day!" But then, I think, if I were wearing my Gold's Gym muscle shirt with their logo on it, I wouldn't have to say anything.

My routine at the gym is to try a variety of cardio and strength training exercises. There are scores of different pieces of equipment to choose from to achieve my goal. I tend to select the easiest ones to use. Just last week I started my routine as usual, thirty minutes on a stationary bike, riding at ten miles as hour at level four. This level, for me, equates to riding five miles on my touring bike in the summer on a rather flat and level road without steep hills to climb. You know the hills, where you have to stand up on the pedals just to make it to the top. The routes I pick are the "easy peasy" ones, as the saying goes.

So, during my last trip to the gym, I'm on my bike, looking around, and in front of me is the weight and power lifting section. I notice a young twenty-something woman putting on a weight lifting belt and beginning to stack large black disk weights on the bar. I notice no unusual popping muscles anywhere as I watch her put three disks on each end of the bar, for a total of six. I'm looking and thinking, that a strong wind would cause her a bit of trouble trying to stand straight up. She's that thin. She clamps the weights on the bar to secure them and walks over to the center of the bar, bends over and snaps it up to her waist and then setting it down on the mat. She repeats this action ten times! After a short rest, she proceeds to lift the bar up to her waist, and then to her neck, and finally, over her head . . . five times! I am amazed! I'm sitting on my bike just wondering what each of those discs weigh? Can't be that much I think to myself because she picks them up and tosses them around so easily.

I keep peddling, take a few more swigs from my water bottle, and soon I've completed my five miles. Heart rate is up, I'm breathing heavier now as I notice the young lady has moved on to another section of the gym. I causally wander over to the weight rack to look at the black disks, and I am amazed to read on each one of them, "Forty-Five lbs."! Let's see, three on each side, six altogether, that's an amazing and unbelievable *TWO HUNDRED AND SEVENTY POUNDS* and I'd guess she didn't weigh an ounce over one hundred and thirty pounds herself. Heck, I struggle to lift and a carry a forty-pound bag of mulch from the trunk of the car to the gardens. I'm wondering what am I missing here, my forty vs. her two hundred and seventy pounds?

The next station for my routine is the shoulder press machine. As I walk toward it, I notice she is at the machine near where I'm headed. I want to stop and tell her how amazed I am at what she was doing with the weights and the amount she was lifting. But then I thought, what would she think of this old Silver Sneakers guy stopping to talk to her? Probably not cool. So I played the scenario over in my head, trying to figure out what I would say to her. The best I could come up with was, "Excuse me, I'm not trying to hit on you, I just couldn't help noticing the weights you were lifting when I was riding the bike, and I am amazed!" Then I quickly thought, she might think I was stalking her, which in itself would be very weird and freaky, so I decided not to say anything and simply to avoid her.

So that's why now I'm telling you, and only you, what happened at the gym today.

My London Bridge Falls Down

Today, I attended my Physical Therapy (PT) session with Lindsay in a place with an interesting name: Orthopedic Sports/Spine Rehabilitation. Interesting names also attend the activities inside.

First I begin with a series of stretches, the technical term being Sciatic Slider, then add to that thirty Bridges. Not like when I was a kid and it was, "London Bridge is falling down." No, these Bridges dictate that I lie on my back with my knees bent, feet flat on the floor, my arms at my side, while pulling my belly button in and up towards my spine. Then, as if attached to some imaginary rope hanging from the rafters, I must try to pull my tummy up and hold that position for ten seconds. Repeat ten times until my bridge does feel like falling down. Oh yes, one other point while doing this, and it is important, Lindsay tells me. I must tighten my butt as I increase the distance I lift my hips off the table.

And this is going to make my back feel better?

Next is Dead Bug. I'm already feeling dead, I tell Lindsay. She just smiles, and those big brown eyes suggest she has heard it all before. "Don't bother getting up" she says, as Dead Bug begins in the same position as the London Bridge which I just finished. So now for Dead Bug. My butt is squeezed tight and high in the air, but now, pure torture is added: "Lift one leg up and stretch it straight out and hold that position for fifteen seconds and then repeat with the other leg. Ten times!"

And so it continues with thirty Clam Shells on each side, twenty Bird Dogs, twenty Front Planks, ten Hurdle Steps, and ten Clock Steps. Lindsay demonstrates all of these for me and follows up supervising closely to make sure I am doing them correctly. And just to be sure that I do them the right way at home, she hands me illustrated print-outs to take with me so I can practice.

I've been doing PT for several weeks. She never asked me if I was practicing at home. She didn't need to. I must confess to you that at the very beginning, I did skip practice at home and justified it to myself that it was OK since Charlotte and I were going to the gym on a regular basis and also working with Maryellen, our personal trainer.

My second week with Lindsay began like this, "We are going to work on your balance and your lumbar region today. So why don't we start with thirty Bird Dogs, and follow that up with ten Front Planks, and thirty Front Clock Steps and thirty Side Clock Steps, and then I have some balance exercises to show you today." I stood there looking kind of silly and sheepish and Lindsay said, "Would you like me to show you how to do them?" I was busted right there on the spot.

That's the week when practice at home began.

The Tattoo

On my way to Gold's Gym in the morning, I usually go through the drive-in at Micky D's and treat myself to a large coffee. On this one particular wonderful, cool, autumn morning, my spirits were high. Peering at the menu board and the little wire screen covering the speaker, I placed my order. From the intercom, a warm, delightful, polite and sweet voice responded, "Is that all?" "Yes," I said, adding, a very warm-hearted, "Thank You!" "That will be a dollar and seventy-two please. First window, please," was the response.

I rounded the corner, lowered my window, and as I drove forward to the cashier's open window, I noticed the young lady was busy on her headset taking the next order of the person behind me in the line of cars. I also noticed the long and colorful tattoo on her arm. She slid her window open, and I blurted out, "You have a flower growing up your arm!" "Yes, you noticed," she responded. Feeling a bit embarrassed now with my smart-mouth forwardness, I continued, "I like it. It is beautiful." And with that comment, I was being totally honest. She replied with the sweetest "Thank you," accompanied by a smile as wide as the Pacific Ocean is from the Atlantic across this great land of ours.

As I drove away, that one flower tattoo seemed to be burned in my mind, and I couldn't concentrate or think of much of anything else for the rest of the day. What bothered me was the question I kept asking myself. If I ever had the courage to get a tattoo, would I hide it? Where would I put it? And what would it be? A flower with a long stem, perhaps a Herbstsonne? With leaves or not? A clever or cute saying like, "Fish and visitors stink after three days." Maybe a quotation? To make one think or question my choice, I'd try: "Eat well, stay fit, die anyway!" A four leaf clover (in dark green) or maybe ivy, or a grape vine in Kelly green? A name like William J. Shakespeare? No doubt there would be many inquiries about the *J.*, sort of like my comment earlier that morning at Mickey D's. A significant date or number perhaps? I wonder if this would work: 3.1415926535? This would no doubt lead someone to comment on my tattoo or at least, question, why? An animal might work. Perhaps a scaly pangolin. A rendering of Big Foot might be interesting, in a furry brown. Why stop there? How about a terrapene or a cockle shell to represent our friends from the sea?

I would never get a tattoo. It is just the thought of, "If I did, what would it be and where would I commit to having it inked in glorious color on my body?" Maybe on the sole of my left foot? Or not!

WHAT FOLLOWS WINTER?

As memories of childhood and young pre-teen years float through my head, I find myself thinking of finding that perfect snowdrift. Cloaked in heavy wool outer garments while searching for it, I was so protected from the cold, snow, and wind that if I slipped or tripped and fell down, I could not get up without one of my playmates helping me to stand. We searched for not just any ole run-of-the mill snowdrift mind you, but the perfect one, formed by the wind blowing across the open field, the drift piled high by the wind on the lee side of the big round hay bale, the ideal drift that was covered by sleet during the night and had the perfect crust. It made for excellent tunneling with shovels and for creating an open doorway to the hollowed out igloo that was just the right size to allow my cousin and me into the safe and warm interior, protected from the blowing west wind. For me, it is a winter wonderland memory.

I also remember blizzards, when the heights of the drifts in our driveway were even with the roof of the car. After several hours of shoveling to free the car from the snow, we would then be able to open the door to see if the car would start. When it did not, opening the hood revealed the hidden reason: it was the packed snow that filled the engine bay cavity completely, from the fire wall to radiator from one side to the other. I also recall the time I thought I'd become rich by shoveling many of the neighbors' driveways at $5 each. Things were going quite nicely until one neighbor, directly across the street from our house, agreed that I could shovel his driveway for him. I wasn't thinking clearly that day and didn't realize he had a sunken driveway leading to his garage under the family room of their split-level home. It was the only home of this type in our entire neighborhood. Each of my shovelfuls had to be tossed at least eight feet high from the paved surface to the top of the snowbank I had created to clear the way. I should have kept and framed that Lincoln as a reminder to never do that again!

Thoughts of the word *winter* have several different meanings for folks. Which leads me back directly back to the question raised in the title, what follows winter?

I am not the first to compare life with the seasons of the year. Traditionally, winter is usually thought of as pretty much the endgame. I would rather think of it as late adulthood, a term used by the German-American psychologist Eric Erickson in the late 20th century. In my opinion, there are way too many negative connotations built around the winter of our lives, as terms usually associated with it are *sadness*, *heartbreak*, *loneliness*, and *sickness*. I've had a little bit of my fair share of sickness; however, I would like to think of the winter of my life in terms of establishing my own identity, caring for others, generosity, understanding my life and its purpose, having a sense of dignity, enjoying intimate relationships, and just practicing loving.

I like Erickson's categories of the various stages of life. The infant/toddler stage is the spring of our lives where we have new beginnings, opportunities, endless hope, deep curiosity, and a time for new things or experiences.

Summer is our next season. Erickson classifies it as adolescence, learning/schooling. I think the summer of our lives is filled with growth, joy, and almost endless exuberance. It was the time when I became somewhat aware of myself, that is who I am as a person and what I could strive to be. At this stage of my life, I was learning how to form friendships, many of which turned out to be rather short lived and a few that have lasted through the years.

Erickson identifies the stage when summer transitions into fall as young, middle, and adulthood. I think part of adulthood for me was experiencing some success and achievements and also learning from the many mistakes I made in my chosen career. It was also a time of continuing to make social and personal connections and to experience the joy, love, and establishment of bonding with others and reaping excitement from those connections and interactions.

As fall slowly morphs into winter and the daylight hours shorten, darkness envelops us for longer periods of time. Sadness, heartbreak, loneliness, sickness, can overtake some folks who live in these tight spaces of late adulthood. This is the final stage of life as identified in Erickson's work and writings. In my mind, I feel it is a time of enjoying the intimate and lifelong relationships that I have made. It is the time in my life when I feel I can begin to reflect on and to understand the purpose of life. It is now my time to care, be generous in thought and deed, live with dignity, and love in the deepest sense and meaning of the word. Also a time to think, but not dwell, on what follows the winter of my life. I may not remember each and every day, but I cherish the memories and time spent with family and my life-long soul mate and friend, Charlotte, with my deepest love and gratitude.

What is life?

Confucius:

Life is really simple, but we insist on making it complicated.

Cesare Pavese:

We do not remember days. We remember moments.

Dalai Lama:

Our prime purpose in this life is to help others. And if you cannot help them, at lease do not hurt them.

Marie Curie:

Nothing in life is to be feared; it is only to be understood. Now is the time to understand more, so we may fear less.

William James:

The greatest use of life is to spend it on something that will outlast it.

William Morris:

> The true secret of happiness lies in taking a genuine interest in all the details of daily life.

My thought of what life is is that it is unfair for many, blessed for a few, and regardless of the circumstances of where or when or how you were born, to be lived fully each and every day with the realization that this dream may not be achieved by everyone.

That igloo in the snowdrift I recall from my childhood was warm inside and protected me from the harrowing winter winds. That feeling of being safe and protected during the winter storm remains with me today. And as my aunt calls us in for lunch from playing in our newly created warm spot in the cave, do we really have to go? When she hollers out the back door of the farmhouse, "Gary, Dale, it's time for lunch, now!" do we make believe we did not hear her?

Do you have any choice when you are called home?

Happy Birthday!

Birthdays have always been significant celebrations for our family and are especially important and meaningful to my spouse, Charlotte. On a few occasions, I wished to make her special day one of remembrance and sought to find unique surprises and experiences to present to her.

One such activity was to drive her to a location out in the country to a mining operation and wish her a Happy Birthday deep underground. Specifically, 1,100 feet underground!

At this time we were living and working in the North Country in New York State, and the Belmont mining operations were fairly nearby. I made arrangements for us to visit the mine. We rode the same elevator that the miners use to go underground for their work shifts and descended to the main tunnel which was named Level 1. From this area we were able to descend to the deepest level of the mine but had to be accompanied by the superintendent of the mine. Once we reached the deepest level and were told we could go no further. From there, I was able to wish her a Happy Birthday deep underground. Perhaps this was one of her special B-Days that I hoped she would remember. But then, each one is special, isn't it?

For yet another birthday celebration, I had made arrangements for a flight. Not just any flight nor any airplane, but a flight in a replica

World War I open cockpit bi-wing. Take off and landings were to be made on a rather short grass runway lined with barrels to guide the pilot in his position on the field. There was no control tower or building for passengers, just what was left of a farm and its pastures from years past. The plane had two seats. The passenger sat in the front seat while the pilot sat in the back where the controls were located. Due to the noise from the engine and the sound of the rushing wind in the open cockpit when in the air, very little communication was able to take place unless one was to shout loudly over the sound of the engine and the rushing wind. Once back on the ground after landing, I wished her a joyous and a Happy Birthday. I hoped she heard me because her ears were still ringing.

After a couple of years had passed, another birthday was to be celebrated with another flight, but this one was planned to be a different experience. Charlotte had an interest in seeking a pilot's license, so arrangements were made for a flying lesson. She flew with her instructor while I stayed on the ground and observed. This particular lesson was practicing take-offs and landings in a modern fixed-wing aircraft. It was a beautiful and clear day and her takeoff was excellent in my opinion from my vantage point. There were a few more practice runs made, and the gentleman standing next to me struck up a conversation which went something like this:

Stranger: Who are you observing today?

Me: My wife.

Stranger: Is she taking a lesson?

Me: Yes, practicing take-offs and landings!

Stranger: Looks like she is coming in for another landing right now. Yes, looks like she is lining up with the runway right now.

Me: Yes, I think you're right. She is!

Stranger: We're not going to be able to see her touch down because that hangar will block our view. Want to go over there so we can see better?

Me: I don't think we have enough time to run over there before she lands.

Stranger: Here she comes. Looks like she's coming a little too high and a little too fast.

Me: She's behind the hangar. I can't see her now.

Stranger: There she is! She just landed!

Me: I couldn't tell if she was too fast, but she's landed OK and is almost stopped! Beautiful!

I walk over to where the plane is stopped near the hangar to greet her and exclaim, "That was amazing! Happy Birthday, and how was the landing?"

Now I know not to use the words *landing* and *birthday* in the same sentence as they may deter the meaning of the word *happy*.

THE REST OF THE STORY

For this tale, let's just call the protagonist, George. I was hired by George to be the new high school principal, and soon after I joined the district, I began to hear whispers from so many folks. Quietly and under their breath, they would refer to him as "crazy George." In my opinion, he wasn't crazy but I admit perhaps a bit eccentric, unusual, different, or any one of several terms meant not to offend folks who "marched to the beat of a different drum."

George's entire career and tenure was in just this one district. He began his career as the high school science teacher, responsible for all the science courses, then served as the principal, and became and remained the superintendent until he retired after many years in that position. Many if not all the members of the board of education were, at one time, his former students. I worked for and reported to him for just one year before he decided to retire. It was a poverty-stricken area and a very poor school district. The years that George worked there, he focused on keeping costs as low as possible, helping and aiding the community, children, and residents in every way. Perhaps a few of these times, his assistance and aid methods were rather creative, unusual, and unorthodox. I was hired by the board of education and followed George as the new superintendent. It was a steep learning curve for me to understand the unorthodox accounting methods. I am reminded of my first year in the position when the district had to file the annual reports for state aid, and I realized the record reflected we were busing more students than were enrolled in the school! That "mistake" was addressed on the first state aid form that was filed and that I had to sign.

During my first year in working and reporting to George, the district was notified that state auditors would be arriving on a specific date and were planning to stay for a few days to examine the bus garage and transportation records, mileage reports, and capacity statistics. Prior to the arrival date, somehow the file drawers in the bus garage office file cabinets "broke" and all the papers fell to the floor, then had to be picked up and put in cardboard boxes and taken to the conference room where the auditors were scheduled to work. Of course the dated files were no longer in any type of sequential order. The auditors' scheduled three-day visit lasted into the second week and then they finally left very frustrated and not totally being able to complete their assigned task.

George had a very old Ford truck he loved to drive, and he used it for trips to the garbage dump, hauling wood for heating his home, driving to the woods for hunting, and many trips around town. One of his famous tricks which he loved to pull on unsuspecting victims involved his steering wheel. When he was driving down the road slowly, he would pull up on the steering wheel with both hands, and it would come off the steering column very easily, and then he would hand it to his passenger and say, "Now you drive!" He thought it was the funniest thing in the world. If you did not know about his sense of humor or his trick, you no doubt found it scary, crazy, and not the least bit funny. Of course you would not accept a ride from George after the first one, and somehow you were the person always offering to drive both of you to a meeting out of town. I wonder why?

In days long gone, New York State had a warehouse in Albany where all kinds of surplus materials were stored, and school districts could visit and take any items they could use. With huge budgets for state offices in Albany, the latest office furnishings were ordered, and the old furnishings were sent to the warehouse. Of course, the proper paperwork had to be filed first, approved, and an appointment date set for such a visit.

George made many visits to the warehouse over the years. He would drive the district's service truck himself. Tales circulated for years about what George did for his community. Some years it was furniture and items for the school such as wooden desks for teachers for their rooms or lounge, old typewriters, tables, waste baskets, office equipment, chairs, fans, anything you can imagine was delivered back to the school with each truck load. Other trips would include older or outdated materials ordered for state workers but not used, such as rubber work boots, rain and wool jackets, hats, sweaters, shirts, gloves, sanitarium or jail blankets, sheets, and the list goes on and on.

Upon returning back to town, George would get the word out to the residents to come to the school on a specific date and time and it would be like Christmas. Families now had winter clothes, hats, gloves, boots, etc., to stay warm and dry. One of George's trips included numerous cross-cut two man saws, no doubt excess or unused from the state's forestry school/program or road crews before the advent of chain saws.

When I became superintendent, I inherited much surplus left-overs that did not find a use in the district or community. Did I mention my task of trying to rid the district of various sizes of tires, rope, chain, and soaps? Well a grade sale works wonders! All my observations and interactions lead me away from the label of "crazy George," directly to a caring and soft-hearted George. No matter what your conclusions may be, George lives on in the minds and folklore of the old timers and in my mind also. I just checked and I'm pleased to share with you, sweet George is still enjoying life in Florida! I don't know if he still has his old Ford truck for tricks.

I was appointed superintendent and then the calendar date arrived and it was George's very last day in the district before his retirement. As I remember that day it seemed to go like this with George always being the jokester.

George: Well Gary, I wish you the best! Just in case of trouble, I left a sealed letter in the top desk drawer for you. Only open it in an emergency and save the stamp. (George was a stamp collector).

Me: Well, George, I wish you the very best in your retirement.

George: I'm not going anywhere. I'll be right here in town. Oh, by the way, if you ever need a substitute teacher for science, I'm available!"

Me: (Thought to myself, *oh no!*)
                 Take care, good friend!

George: I hope you don't mind if I stop in before school starts to have a cup of coffee with you?

(*Oh no, I thought to myself, he's going to bug me about running the district. He's going be here all the time. I don't want to babysit him.*)

I did not see George in school once that summer, but a few days before the opening of the school year, George appeared in my doorway, unannounced of course!

George: I'm here for that cup of coffee you promised me.

Me: Hi, George! Come in, please, and grab a chair.

George: Aren't you going ask me what I'm doing here?

Me: George, what brings you to school today?

George: Kindergarten registration!

Me: Tell me more.

George: I'm here to register our son for kindergarten!

Me: Are you joking?

George: No.

And so it turned out to be the true situation. I did not know that George and his first and only wife had a five year old son! I had worked for him for a year and had an invitation to his home once for a dinner! I knew and dealt with his 16-year-old son who was in high school but never knew about the younger son.

My first year we did lose the chemistry teacher, who resigned to take a position in industry. We needed a sub on short notice, and George was hired as a substitute teacher for a short period of time and approved by the board of education.

FASTEN YOUR SEATBELT

Friends who know me, realize that all mechanical things like cars, motorcycles, trucks and all gasoline-engine-powered conveyances have been my passion and a source of enjoyment during my lifetime. Over many years, I have no doubt accumulated, owned, worked on, and driven more than 50 different vehicles. Now that may sound like a lot of expenditures, but I assure you that most of them were considered "junk" or "used up" by their previous owners. What this translates to is that they were very inexpensive for me to purchase and to be included in my ownership in the early years of my youth and young adulthood.

One of the recent additions to my garage collection is a 1974 Cadillac Eldorado. This particular vehicle is a two-door luxury car produced by General Motors and was a classic symbol of American luxury during the 1970s. In a word, it was opulent. It is powered by a hefty 8.2 liter V-8 engine that equates to 500 cubic-inch displacement, all of which means it is big, fast, and powerful. In short, a monster compared to the cars of today. It has a total length of a massive 224 inches, which makes it more than 18 and a half feet long! And so it is commonly referred to as a "land yacht" or quite simply, "a monster." Very often it was also referred to as a mafia car. When sold new, with options that were available at the time, the price, converted to today's dollars, was about $60,000.

It is not an economy car by any stretch of the imagination as it was designed purely as a luxury car. Few, if any of the elite owners were concerned about economy or mileage. If you are very careful when you drive it, you may be able to get 13 or 14 miles per gallon of gas! I only use it on special occasions and for unique outings, such as driving it to car shows and events. It is a rather rare car to be seen on the highways today; however, almost everyone recognizes that it is an older classic car, and it is rather unique.

One rather unusual feature of the car is that it was designed by GM engineers to meet a new federal mandate. That new law required that henceforth seatbelts were mandatory and must be used by the driver and the front seat passenger. It was the only GM automobile designed that year to ensure the law was enforced. For the period of this one year, the 1974 Cadillac required its owner to have his or her seatbelt fastened before the car could even be started. This is commonly referred to as an inner locking device and was electronically controlled. It was not a popular design. For example, in the event that you wanted to move your car ahead a few feet in your driveway after leaving it to go into the house or garage, you had to settle back in and buckle up before you could even start the car. Owners were soon frustrated by the inconvenience, and so this design feature only lasted one year.

After I acquired this car and after the first year of owning it, a gasoline leak was discovered and was traced to the sender on the top of the fuel tank. To be repaired, it meant that the tank had to be drained of all the gas in it and then removed from the car for the part to be replaced. It was a large task that I did not want to undertake as I no longer wished to be climbing under cars to repair them. I was getting too old for that nonsense, and my body told me that, so I thought it best to pay attention.

I took the car to my good friend Mike, who owns King's Auto Repair garage in our town and asked him if he would do me a favor and fix my problem. He agreed, and so I left the car for him to work on. It took a quite a while before the new part could be located and shipped from the vendor. Due to lack of storage space in his building, he decided to put the car outside and park it in the lot behind his garage.

When I went to pick up the car after he called me and said it was ready, he also mentioned that he had some good news and bad news. When I arrived and went into the office to pay the bill, he handed me a new set of car keys complete with the Cadillac insignia and said, "You may need these to drive it home." Now I was curious and inquired of Mike, "What's this all about?"

While the car was parked outside and waiting for the new parts to arrive, apparently someone during the night tried to steal it. They broke into the car and tried to start it by removing the ignition switch from the steering column and hot wiring it. Remember my words about those GM engineers who were going to be sure that the driver was going to follow the law and put their seatbelt on for safety reasons? Well, I am grateful to those very engineers, whoever they may be, because do you think that if someone was going to steal your car, that they would make sure they had their seatbelt on before trying to start it? Well, apparently that's exactly what happened in this situation as the thieves were not concerned at all with having their seatbelt on while driving a stolen car. And so they could not get it started to make their getaway!

RED FLAGS

Charlotte and I had planned a six-week road trip through Portugal, Spain, and France. As a part of making this trip become a reality, we contacted our travel agent and requested his assistance. We had called him many times in the past for our travel destinations in Europe, so we felt comfortable in contacting him again. As a part of our initial discussions, we indicated our desire to travel through these countries by driving our own rental car as we had done so many times prior, so our agent began his research for us. We had used a company named Auto Europe on previous trips and were pleased with them, so our agent made his first inquiries with this same company. Auto Europe indicated that they would be able to assist us with our special request, which was to pick up a car in Portugal, drive around Portugal and Spain, and drop it off at the end of our journey in France, from where we would take our flight home. Since this was a rather unusual request, our agent sent me the following email after completing his thorough search:

I've found a great lease program for non–EU residents running over 30 days in Europe. They are offering a Peugeot 308, with standard transmission, for $1,762 including taxes, collision, fire, and liability insurance, a GPS, VAT tax-exempt, plus a free second driver. Pick up and drop off would be at depots (very similar to our regular rental locations). In order to book, I need to give them your credit card information, and it will be processed in 2 to 3 business days. Please let me know if this meets your needs.

I indicated that this sounded fine, not paying any attention to the word *lease* after I read "very similar to our regular rental locations." A few weeks later I began to receive a batch of paperwork from Auto Europe. Many of the forms were in French with no English translation to accompany the documents. At about the same time, I also received the following from our agent:

In the next few weeks, I will receive paperwork for the lease for you to fill out and return. We will need to make an appointment for you to pick up and drop off the car.

Hindsight is a very interesting thing. After we had completed this trip, which turned out to be an outstanding experience and everything went fairly well. Where it did not go well, looking back, I should have noticed these "red flags" along with the word *lease* in the communication:

"Rental company: Peugeot."

"Auto Europe does not provide insurance."

"Coverage is provided by Peugeot."

"No on-site office."

"No location for pick up."

"You will need to make an appointment for pick up and drop off."

"Special instructions apply."

"TT Car Transit Agent."

"Registered in France."

"I put you in for your *lease*. It works a little differently than a car rental."

"They will request the car from Peugeot and get a confirmation."

"In the next few weeks, I will receive paperwork for the *lease*."

"You to fill out and return as then you will be registered for that car."

"(with no drop-off charge for a different city.)"

At this point I was interchanging the word *rental* and the word *lease* in my mind and not paying attention to "*You will need to make an appointment for pick up and drop off.*" I was thinking, of course I'll call the office when I'm ready to pick up and drop off the car. I always did this before when traveling by rental car.

Our trip turned out to be fantastic! We drove overnight from home to Toronto, Canada, and then the next day flew to Frankfurt, Germany, where we took a train to Oporto, Portugal, where we stayed for three days. We then traveled by train to Lisbon, spent a few days, and then we were to pick up our rental car, which turned out to be a very interesting adventure.

When I phoned the car company, Auto Europe, and inquired as to where we should pick up the car, we were told to meet a gentleman who would be standing outside the parking lot of a specific named hotel near the airport. I was given the name and the street where it was located. After hailing a taxi, I requested that the driver take us to the hotel and told him I was looking for a man with a briefcase, standing outside the parking lot on the street corner. Our taxi driver looked at us with that very puzzled look, and my only thought was *This guy, rightfully so, is thinking, crazy Americans!* After going around the block several times, passing the hotel, we told him we needed to find the guy with a briefcase on the curb standing by the hotel. All our taxi driver kept saying was *fook* as we drove past the hotel several times. At first I had no idea what he was saying, but then it wasn't long before we figured it out. It was at this point that the driver asked me for my slip of paper on which I had written the name of the hotel and the name of the street, and he repeated the same word, and we now understood what he was saying in Portuguese.

The taxi driver drove by the hotel once more and sure enough, there was a man with a briefcase, standing at the corner of a driveway leading into the parking lot of the hotel from the street. The lot was surrounded by a chain-link fence, and all of this seemed to be a bit sketchy to me. Even though this was a bit strange, we drove into the lot and inquired of the man if you could tell us where the office was to pick up a rental car we had reserved. He assured us that there was no auto rental office; however, he was here to take care of us and was expecting us and we were going to pick up our car from him. He then walked over to a new Peugeot 308, put a key into the trunk lock, opened it, and placed his briefcase in the trunk! From his briefcase he took out several papers for me to sign. I signed my name, and he handed me the keys to the car and that was it. No instructions, no details, no check of driver's licenses, no money exchanged, and off we drove. We covered a total of 5,000 kilometers in six weeks as we toured Europe in a new car that was delivered to us with zero kilometers on the odometer.

Then the time came for us to fly home from Paris and back to Toronto. When returning the car to the rental office, yes, the rental office at the airport, the first thing the agent said to me was, "Would you like us to ship your car to the States or would you like us to buy it back from you?" This is exactly where the red flags came in to play. It was at this point that I realized that six weeks prior I had purchased a brand new car, and now I'm standing in front of the agent and signing papers for the Peugeot company to buy it back from me. The only cost involved was my initial deposit, which I thought was the rental fee, but in reality it was the down payment on a brand new car which I had leased and had not rented. I guess from now on, I had better pay closer attention to all the red flags, the details, and the words *rental* and *lease* even if many of them are in French.

BEYOND

In several of my past musings, I have reflected on the fleeting passage of time. I am reminded of Carl Sagan's reference to our earth as that "pale blue dot" in our galaxy. Considering how small the Milky Way galaxy is compared to the other galaxies and that it is just one of the two trillion out there, we are almost lost in space. We are almost lost in time also. Our blue dot makes a complete rotation toward the sun once a day, and as I contemplate the more than thirty thousand such rotations that I have had the pleasure of taking so far during my lifetime, I realize my span here is just a fleeting moment in Pale Blue Dot's existence in the scale of geologic time.

Thinking of time, I reflect on mine here on Pale Blue Dot. When my time is up, I often ponder, what's next? All of us are familiar with that portal from which no one returns and the unknowns associated with it. The best-kept secret is never revealed to us from those who have gone before. We have developed a vocabulary to attempt to deal with the reality that we all must move on and through this portal. Some of the these terms we have coined include: *death, mortality, beyond the grave, nothingness, sleep, lifelessness, demise, deceased, passing, the great divide, exited,* and so on. This unexplored space beyond the portal we must pass only becomes known to us as our journey takes us through our last breath, heartbeat, and thoughts. It

is the mystery of the ages. To be absolutely clear and positive, I am in
no hurry, nor do I have any anxiety about my passage through the
portal. I like it fine where I am currently and enjoy it very much. That
being said, I still think about the journey that I must go on at some
point in time and what I am going to miss by not being here to enjoy.
Some of those things that will be missed include:

- Holding my wife Charlotte close, feeling her warm and soft
  skin, and breathing deeply in her very fragrance.
- Embracing our children, grandchildren, and great-
  grandchildren.
- Rekindling and continuing the old friendships we have
  developed.
- Taking pure pleasure in savoring the smells and tastes of
  lovingly prepared meals with family at holiday or other
  celebrations.
- Sitting quietly and in silence, listening to the rain on the
  windows, blown by the strong winds of the lake's summer and
  winter storms.
- Fresh pies baking in the oven.
- Morning coffee and toast with eggs and bacon sputtering in the
  iron skillet.
- The smell of a newborn babe.
- A summer rain storm with great clasps of thunder that
  brightens the evening sky.

- The smell of popcorn popping in hot sizzling oil on a cold winter's night.
- The aroma of a crackling wood fire at a campsite in the Adirondacks.
- The smell of fudge cooking on the old kitchen's wood stove.
- Crawling into bed just made up with fresh sheets that were dried on the line.
- The smell of just-mowed hay drying in the morning's sun light.
- Hot pancakes covered with melting butter and real maple syrup.

Wait, I have all these now! All I need to do is take the time to appreciate all that is being offered that's around me. Who knows what waits for me beyond the portal? No one ever returns, so it is still a mystery for all of us left behind. What if it were no mystery at all? Wouldn't that be amazing? If beyond the portal, the only sound heard was that of a newborn babe, the only smell detected was that of a wood fire, and the only new taste to be experienced was that of a freshly baked pie? If it were just these few things, I am sure I wouldn't be disappointed!

STATUES AND ARTWORK

Memory Urn for ashes
Lit in the evening hours
Welded steel, powder-coated finish

Dancing Lady
Heavy steel with powder-coated color finish that moves with the wind
Standing next to the sculpture is its creator, and author of this book,
Gary J. Buehler

Aliens
Indoor or outdoor sculpture with oxidized finish,
clear-coated to maintain patina

End table constructed of square steel tubing
and lathe wound spirals with glass top

All steel patio, poolside, or library conversation chair

Many Hands Make Lite Work
Glass and steel serving bowl

Fences and Gates
Sculptured art field display

Who is the Fairest of All?
Sculptured patina, aged copper mirror, acid treated for color

Focal point all steel, constructed and welded sculpture
power-coated protective finish

Do You Believe in Dragons?
All steel, electrified and gas-fitted sculpture
mounted on roof peak of building

Visiting artist demonstration sculpture
Built on site and now located in lobby entrance

Another *Many Hands Make Lite Work*
Steel and glass serving bowl, powder-coated color protective finish

Dinner bell chime
All steel sculpture with pleasant tone and sound

Garden or patio sculpture of welded steel and cast iron

Garden or patio sculpture
All steel working gears welded with
protective clear finish over base colored coat

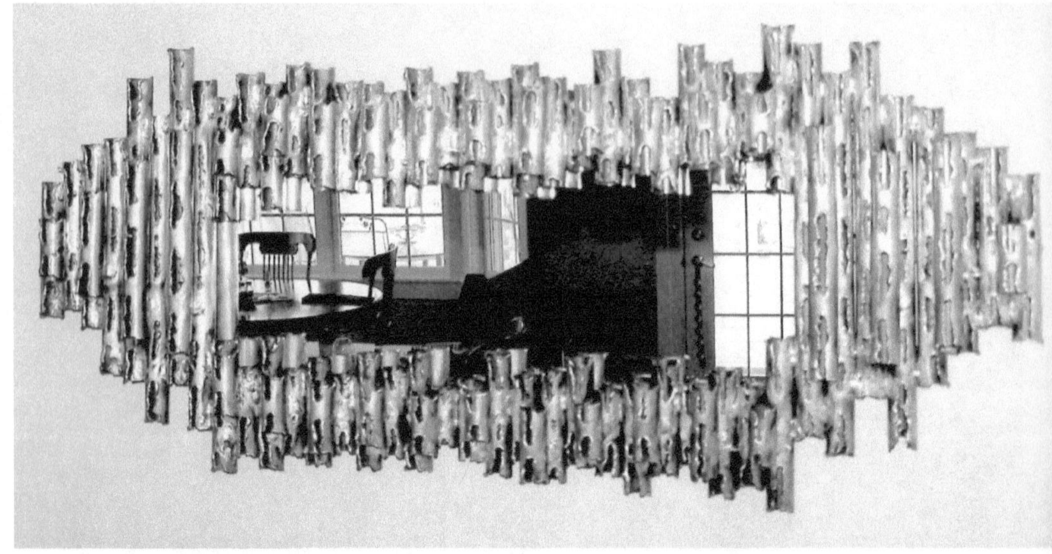

Mirror
Welded steel and brazed copper frame with clear protective coating to prevent any oxidation or change in bright colors over time

Wall hanging
Copper and steel with various acids for colors,
brushed and polished, and sealed with a clear coat

Steel and chrome center focal point sculpture for any setting

Haute Ecole
Plasma cut out of cold rolled steel,
powder coated, solar lit garden sculpture
(48" × 48")